Dedication

*T*his book is dedicated to George Verwer and Dale Rhoton, Co-founders of Operation Mobilization and to their co-workers, who together work tirelessly to spread the Gospel message of hope using pathways on land and sea and air throughout <u>the whole world</u>.

CONTENTS

PART THREE
Questions Driven by Creative Insights

ACKNOWLEDGEMENTS

*T*hanks to Ms. Carol Williamson of the Galilee Gospel Chapel church staff, for her diligent work in typing the manuscript. Her skills in converting my hand-written "scribbles" to readable print are commendable.

Thanks also to fellow Pastor Dr. Keith A. Phillips for reading selections of the draft and for his kind and encouraging words about wide reception of the book.

Preface

*H*ave you ever wondered why we ask so many questions? Please hold on to your answer. This could be your opportunity to explore, experience and enjoy a wonderland of questions.

In my book titled "WHAT ARE YOU THINKING" I invited my readers to stroll with me through an imaginary Thinking Wonderland. During this stroll we (my reader and I) conversed back and forth on the fascinating subject of THINKING. The responses from a wide variety of readers were humbling and touching. Those sincere accolades I will always cherish because I know that my writing was "inspired" and that my contribution to the project was miniscule.

The comments that kept popping up from on-line postings, book signings, and personal chit-chat with my readers were about the discursive nature of the conversation that they felt involved them from the introduction, as we entered the wonderland, to our last steps together before we said good-bye.

These unsolicited comments triggered my initiative to do this follow-up book using a similar conversation format with an equally stimulating and engaging topic – "WHAT IS YOUR QUESTION?" or "DO YOU HAVE A QUESTION?" Whatever you prefer.

To my first time reader, I am sure you will be pleased to share the delight of a stimulating conversation on the topic of QUESTIONS that will be long remembered. The wonderland I referred to earlier, although imaginary, will be like a dream come true. It will be as close as we can get to Sir Arthur's Camelot. There will be breathtaking sunrises, mesmerizing sunsets and azure blue skies with cotton clouds drifting by. There will also be gentle breezes that will adjust to your personal comfort. The only tweetings you will hear will be those in the chorus of hummingbirds, canaries, robins and nightingales.

Although the **wonderland** *is imaginary, the conversation will be a real exchange between your thoughts and mine and should keep us pleasantly engaged until we say good-bye.*

INTRODUCTION

*Y*ou and I are mobile search parties – always asking questions and searching for answers. From our first infant mutterings we babble streams of questions – usually at that stage of infancy we do just that: babble, babble, babble!

If we think back to our childhood days growing up, depending on where we grew up, our parents should be credited for their patience and tolerance with our non-stop, no-sense questions. Now some of us of recent generation are asking more and different questions. We are also aware, or should be, that this present time we call postmodern era, continues to produce seeming endless advances in the human experience because of our questioning instinct. Our growing up period deserves a bit of reflection.

As we grow up, our busy curious 'little' fingers keep pressing a variety of buttons expecting that some kinds of answers will pop up. Sometimes we get answers we like, sometimes not. Sometimes the red warning lights flicker and it seems that the question machine stalls and we get no *answers at all. If we allow for the truth to be told, we will admit that there are questions that we are afraid to ask.*

Ralph Waldo Emerson reminded us that some people are afraid to ask questions because of the fear of what the answers may be. In our adventure into "QUESTION WONDERLAND" we will dismiss any such fears and together explore an assortment of questions about a wide variety of topics.

As we approach the pathway to Question Wonderland, may I mention that there are no ground rules for our conversation, except the expected civility we will accord each other. This way, the conversation will reflect respect for each other's views and opinions. Just to whet your appetite for the scope of questions we will bounce off each other and kick back and forth; we will explore questions related to curiosity (from the time of our ancestors to the present time); we will also explore questions related to challenge (examples and events exemplifying daunting challenges); finally we will explore a variety of questions including those related to personal issues.

Hopefully, as we share this time together we will discover many similarities of curiosity, courage and creativity among our fellow mortals. I can assure you that, if you stay the course, you will be delighted. By the way, I see you are travelling 'light' and so am I! My mini backpack just has room for an item I never leave home without. I thought to bring along one compact book that has all the answers to any question that the human mind can conceive. Want to see my compact reference? No, it's not a dictionary or a compact encyclopedia – it's – you got it! It's a copy of the Good Book - the Holy Bible.

*If you enjoy a relaxed unrehearsed discussion of an interesting variety of topics, you will just love this trip. Your friendly smile gives me such a positive expectation of our exciting trip thru **Question Wonderland.***

Let's go for it!

PART 1

QUESTIONS
DRIVEN BY CURIOSITY

CHAPTER 1

WELCOME TO QUESTION WONDERLAND!

Kick off on the origin of questions

Where were you in the early evening hours of June 15th 2012? Perhaps a better question should be: what were you doing at that time? Perhaps you and I were in the company of several million viewers around the world watching ABC's T.V. presentation of the nail biting daredevil drama featuring Nick Wallenda's tight-cable walk across the roaring Niagara Falls.

From Mr. Wallenda's first precarious step followed by every succeeding nerve-racking step, our collective anxiety elevated to a point where most of us just closed our eyes, especially when he hit a foggy stretch on the cable and was stepping along in blind nervousness – calling out: "Jesus help me!"

There was almost no exception to the question that all of us spectators asked as we exhaled from that hold-our-breath terrifying TV experience. What was that question we asked ourselves? "WHY WOULD ANYONE EVEN THINK OF DOING SUCH A DUMB THING." Well, to Mr. Wallenda, who descends from a daredevil circus performing family the question was not why? But why not? Why not me?

These series of questions were routinely asked by people like, Edmund Hilary (Mt. Everest); Evil Kenevil (crazy motor cycle stunts); Houdini (repeated escape from death traps) and a host of other seeming superhuman beings. Just flip the pages of the Guinness Book of Records and they all come out to greet you with the same chorus of questions why, why not, why not me?

To the point of our questions, or really their questions – not sure Mr. Kenevil knows why he revved up his motorcycle (flying machine) to scale an 80ft wall, breaking 433 bones and miraculously recovered only to go at his antics all over again. Was it for fame? Was it for immortality? Was it for wealth? It certainly was not for health. The questions of "why not" seems to be the birthplace of some of these scary and death-defying capers.

Believe it or not, our thoughtful conversation about questions on curiosity, questions on challenges, and other questions on your menu may give us some insight into our own question and answer make-up. We may be surprised about our capacity for questions and some of our answers. Do you sense that this is going to be a very interesting trip where we can learn from each other and even make some discoveries together? As we make our way through this beautiful display of nature in Question Wonderland - the lush forestry is so inviting – can't escape the obvious thought. What are some questions that come to mind? That's exactly what I am thinking! Where did all this created splendor come from? Where did it start? Who and how? – look at the patterns in the trees as they sway so gracefully in the breeze.

Don't be surprised if we find that we all have a bit of the wonder at nature within us. There is a principle governing all of nature called Finite Continuum. Simply means that everything in our universe that can be measured is finite. ie., everything has a beginning and has an end. There is no exception to this natural law. If we accept that statement of fact, then questions which are part of our everyday experience started somewhere and end at sometime.

I can sense by your quizzical looks that this is a bit of a puzzle. Remember I mentioned earlier that I brought along in my backpack a copy of the Holy Bible that references any subject and answers any questions? This, I think is a good time to get some help in firming up our thinking about all kinds of questions.

So the big question is where did the unique ability to ask all kinds of questions come from? That's a very important question because, I am going to need your help to sort out some very puzzling insights about questions as we continue our stroll in Question Wonderland.

What about the reference I mentioned earlier? Here we go! Funny, how the mind works. As we were about to break out my handy reference, a line from one of my favorite Broadway Musicals – "The Sound of Music" popped into my head. Remember the line that Julie Andrews sings up and down the music scale? "Let's start at the very beginning, Do Re Me -----." <u>Well with that bit of music segue; Let's start at the very beginning</u>. Look, here in the very first book of the Bible – Genesis we have a detailed day-by-day, step-by-step account of the Creation Story.

After a clear and careful chronicle of five (5) days of creation we come to the sixth day (time period) when the Divine Creator God created the first human being and pronounced His final creation act – <u>very good!</u> We read here that He created this man in His image – not <u>identical</u> but with similarities of features. He also created him with distinguishing features: among them thinking apparatus, that cannot be duplicated. The best proof of this statement is really in a brief glimpse of the history of the thinking habits of our fellow mortals and the questions that flowed from their thinking. So far, there is no record anywhere of any device that has ever duplicated the human brain in its uniqueness for <u>originating questions</u>.

In this present millennial generation the questions we pursue and the answers that result will depend upon where we search for these elusive answers.

Now that is a mouthful or you might say a mindful. Well perhaps it's both, and that's why our time together will be full of interesting and stimulating moments. History has favored us with a garden variety of thoughtful questions that continue to tickle our thoughts even as we speak.

CHAPTER 2

EVER HEARD OF JOB?

An ancient man with modern questions

World literature captures and archives for us exceptional people who remain legends in their time as
well as our time. I am sure you have many favorite icons of
history that come to mind on the subject of questions. One
person among the ancient people who has been a household
name for ages is the biblical patriarch named JOB.

By the way, JOB's name pops up frequently when there
is conversation about patience and or unusual adversity.
Over many, many years, even before you and I showed up on
the planet, JOB had a fan club. There are those who argued
fervently on his behalf. His fan club members include some
very sophisticated people who argue for his exceptional
pious life, and ask why should he suffer unjustly? If God is
just, they say, and rewards people who live a clean, upright

righteous life as JOB did, why did God allow this man to suffer so bitterly and so mercilessly? What is your take on the very controversial and puzzling situation about JOB? Give it some thought, no hurry. You say you heard a little bit about JOB in one of your social conversations on Middle Eastern Civilization and also about him from the Bible?

Interesting that you should say that because I had a spirited discussion with a so-called middle-eastern expert. This learned gentleman held his ground in defense of JOB, who in his eyes, did not deserve this tragic experience. His question to me was: why do you think this pious, exceptionally upright man suffered as he did?

We will talk more about JOB's "bad break" later but for now let's defer the topic. Let's talk a bit about questions that, JOB asked instead of questions asked about him. The most exhaustive information about this paragon of patience in suffering and resilience from devastation is found – where do you think? You got that right! The Bible. In the Bible, here take a look, (Job 14:1)

"Mortals, born of woman, are of few days and full of trouble."

We have a blow by blow account of JOB's life and times. Before we get to his questions, let's notice why JOB has captured the attention of people throughout the ages. He was a very astute observer of his "universe." He observed and thought about what he saw as the realities of life and living. JOB was among the first old-timer to observe that trees (plants) have hope. They can spring to life again, even if they are cut down and their roots seem dead in the soil. If they are refreshed by water – they will sprout again!

JOB's silent curiosity made him wonder, how come? How can a tree cut down and seem dead can be revived and sprout again taking its place among other living trees. Then our master observer (JOB) took a close and curious look at women bearing children and wondered if there might be some similarities between plant life and human life. Now look at the question he raised as stated in this 14th verse of the 14th Chapter: "If a man die, shall he live again ---?" In this historic question – JOB modeled for us **the essence of curiosity**, that drives most of our questions.

Before we switch from showcasing JOB as one of the key originators of questions, let's look at another observation that led to that same question. Here is the observation: all human beings came from the womb of a woman (natural birth). A child grows to adulthood and during this lifetime, without exception there is some kind of trouble. This life at some pre-appointed point comes to an end. It seems that the end is but a change from one form of life to another. Those are JOB's observations about human life. His curiosity? Does the "man" die and disappear forever or does he live again? – somewhere, somehow? Curious question isn't it? Thanks Mr. JOB we will be back to pick-up on this specific aspect of your **curiosity**.

CHAPTER 3

CURIOSITY THE MOTHER OF QUESTIONS

Why do we ask so many questions?

I s there any truth to the saying that curiosity kills the cat? Oh these folksy sayings that have been handed down to us as legacies from our parents' generations. Do you think they made them up or do you think they actually observed a curious cat, or two, meeting untimely exists? In other words did they see what curiosity did to some real cats?

Unlike the "proverbial cat" whose curiosity sometimes ends in demise, we are all motivated by boundless curiosity. We are propelled by an innate instinct of our curious nature that defies even imminent demise. The distinguishing features of our curiosity are the questions we raise that are unique to us as human beings. Before we talk further about questions that are driven by our human curiosity we should ask - what is this curiosity that fills every vacuum in our thoughts? Earlier we noticed that questions come from our 'uniqueness' as rational beings. But what is this curiosity that drives these questions? Did you ever really ask yourself for a definition of this curiosity? I'd like to hear your thoughts first. -- You are kidding -- you can't be stumped by a question like that!

Here is how I go at it. I say that we live in a world of all kinds of things and people. We don't know where all these things and people come from and how they really work. In short we really don't understand how the world works. So my take on curiosity is this: <u>it is the urge of my ignorance that prompts me to ask</u>: why, how, what, where, who etc. So there is <u>my home-made version of curiosity</u> that drives the questions that skip in and out of my thoughts.

You say what? You agree with that simplistic version of curiosity? Since you agree this opens up the lid of a whole Pandora's box of questions that our forebears asked. They did not understand so many puzzling things in nature all around them. They did not understand life in their day-by-day experience, but their curiosity questions were endless.

Before we kick around some really interesting questions, just take a look at the casual clothes and shoes we are wearing - jeans and sneakers, providing us with skin protection and body comfort. Our ancestors certainly did not dress up in fancy clothes and footwear. It seems that after generations of suffering the stings of insects and pesky bites of bugs,

they asked themselves some pretty common sense questions
- what can we do to protect the largest organ of our bodies -
our skin? So that's what clothes are for you ask - seriously?
You would never guess when you look at some of the outfits
that we now call the latest styles. Sometimes do you catch
yourself asking - what in the world is that "get up" people are
wearing? Good question.

Remember a moment ago we were saying that human
curiosity from the earliest times started driving questions,
that spread like wild fire in an open field of straw. These questions started from basic survival needs, like what to eat and/
or drink safely? These may seem basic and unnecessary but
they were necessary for the survival of our ancestors. Many,
many tens of thousands of people perished because these
survival-type questions were not answered in the affirmative.

We have not paid attention or given enough credit to those
who preceded us who year after year, decade after decade,
century after century, kept pursuing answers to those questions. They questioned this, and they questioned that. They
tried this and they tried that, in stubborn and relentless survival efforts even against unimaginable odds. Why were they
doing this? That's right! They had us in mind, they felt that
the survival questions they left unanswered, the next generation would pick up and run with them like passing the baton
in a track and field relay race that would keep on going.

These intrepid ancestors of ours never gave up. They cor-
rectly felt that somewhere in the lengthy stretches of time,

answers would come to their <u>curiosity- driven questions</u>. We owe these curiosity-driven-questioning forebears a huge debt of gratitude. They were not quitters. Their questions kept coming even when they did not get all the answers they were searching out. They did not quit and so shouldn't we.

CHAPTER 4

CURIOSITY QUESTIONS UNLIMITED

What's up there in the heavens above us?

L et's pry a bit further into curiosity driven questions. I am sure that you have quite a few of those questions up your sleeves.

Let's think about this. In a quiet moment, have you thought how special and unique we fellow mortals are? What about how unique and special is this dwelling place where we share temporary space? Yes I am referring to planet earth – this amazing cosmic mystery.

Just think of this tiny bit of cosmic "trivia." There is a line in an old favorite hymn that says: "let every kindred, every tribe on this terrestrial ball, hail Him who saves you by His grace and crown Him Lord of all!" Did you catch the part about this terrestrial ball? I thought we must be really special and unique to be riding around in this vast expanse of space on this terrestrial carousel we call earth, without having to pay a single penny for the ride.

Are you asking me what was that cosmic trivia I mentioned so casually? You picked upon that comment. That makes me think that you are really tuned in. I was really thinking that we are daily surrounded by so much mystery, so much we don't and can't understand. What's that you ask? Think about this ball shaped piece of real estate we call planet earth, where you and I share comfortable space. I am thinking and asking this curious question: How is it that earth is just the right shape, and the right weight, and the right distance from the sun and has the right volume of water (fresh and salt), and the right combination of chemicals in the air and on its land surface, and the only known such place in all the billions of constellations in all of the universe with all the precise elements for life support?

By the way on this unique piece of real estate there exists <u>as no where else</u>, all the resources to sustain human life. Think of the approximate seven (7) billion dwellers of every tribe and nation and for all the changing seasons of all these years of time past and the rest of our limited time. Think of the creative genius that originated and keeps this system – "Life on earth" sustained. Talk about chance. How is that for chance? Think of that question!

Speaking of time past – our ancestors never stopped looking around and up above. The heavens have always, from the earliest times, triggered their curiosity and questions long, long before there was any concept of dedicated study of the "heavens" above us, these were effusive expressions of awe, mystery and grandeur that left these stargazers breathless. Do you remember King David, one of Israel's great kings, who wrote repeatedly about his fascination with the heavenly bodies. In one of his expressions (Psalms) here are his words: take a look, Psalm 8 says

"O Lord, our Lord, how excellent is thy name in all the earth! Who hast set thy glory above the heavens. Out of the mouth of babes and sucklings hast thou ordained strength because of thine enemies, that thou mightiest still the enemy and the avenger. When I consider thy heavens, the work of thy fingers, the moon and the stars, which thou hast ordained; what is man, that thou art mindful of him? and the son of man, that thou visitest him?"

Did you sense that King David was raising a great question? Did you ever think of David's curiosity behind his question – "what is man that you are mindful of him?" In other words, why is this great creator God paying attention to human beings on planet earth? Why are we so special to God that we attract his attention and deserve his blessings? King David was transfixed by celestial curiosity, are you? I am! I am more than ever. The more I learn about the nature of the universe, the more I am lost in the adoration of <u>our</u> <u>Great Creator</u>. Ever heard this song about the Great Creator? Goes like this:

"Down from His Glory, ever living story, my God and Savior came and Jesus was His Name, the Great Creator became my Savior and all God's fullness were met in Him."

Isn't it funny how I remember the words that many years ago I heard church people singing so cheerfully? These words caught my attention but not my interest. That was then. What about now? Well, now I'm like King David, I have gotten past the curiosity of why a Great Creator would be mindful of mankind. I have the personal experience of knowing this Great Creator as my personal Savior and that has opened up for me a whole <u>new world of faith and hope</u>! You seem interested by your facial expression. If you are, we can pick up on this later. I'll share with you how I reached this point in my life's journey.

CHAPTER 5

LOOKING UP AND LOOKING AROUND

Questions looking for answers?

As far back as we can search in the archives of man's history, long, long, before the invention of the wheel or the discovery of writing tools – paper and pen etc., we find our ancestors looking around and gazing up into the mysterious reaches of space – the heavens. They have never lost their fascination for this display of majesty and mystery we call – the universe. It seems that we have inherited some levels of their fascination. Perhaps it's in our genes – maybe. This fascination has been so extreme that some ancient culture like the Egyptians worshipped the sun, which they thought to be the God of the heavens. They thought of all those twinkling stars as heavenly dominions ruled by the rising and setting sun.

Do you enjoy gazing up into the starry heavens when the night sky is ablaze with twinkling stars that seem so far away and yet so near? When I was growing up, there were so many delightful little jingles that were floating around that some of them seem to stick in my mind. One I remember, as we are on the subject of stars in the heavens is: "Twinkle, twinkle little stars, how I wonder what you are. Up above the world <u>so high</u> like a diamond <u>in the sky</u>." It's almost automatic, as we look up to the heavens that we become fascinated and filled with admiration and wonder.

Even if the heavens seem so impossibly out of reach and the cosmos seem beyond our boundaries of thought, <u>our curiosity is unstoppable,</u> so are the questions that emerge. Do you wonder what was the National Air and Space Administration (NASA) label attached to our latest super space probe that landed on Mars on August 12th, 2012? What do you recall? Yes! You got that exactly right. No one could miss the message. It is labeled: **CURIOSITY**. That is the purpose and mission of this super ingenious project of science and engineering. Yes, they named this latest rover (probe) **CURIOSITY**.

Why is this NASA robotic spectacular crawling at a snail's pace, probing around the surfaces of Mars and drilling into the core of the Red Planet as we speak? You've got the answer at your fingertips. That's right – they want to find answers to their <u>compelling curiosity-driven questions.</u> Can we human beings live on this uninhabited planet? We are curious! If not, why not? That is exactly why we are spending billions of dollars extracted from United States taxpayers to fund this Curiosity Project. Is this Red Planet (Mars) our next door neighbor, a place where we humans can land and find the reception and hospitality accorded to the present robotic visitor?

The probe **CURIOSITY** as well as its prior Mars visitors named: **Sojourner**, **Opportunity** and **Spirit** have not given us the answers.

As we are speaking, our ingenious robotic probe (Rover) is sending back data to NASA from the surface of Mars – approximately 50 million miles out in space. You think this is earth-shaking news – wait till you hear the latest piece recently reported by the New York Times Science Section. The summary of the piece is this: a non-profit group based in Holland launched a project to land humans on Mars by 2024-25. They released news that 200,000 applicants have signed on for a <u>one-way ride to Mars</u>. This number of applicants has been reduced to about 1,000 and will be further reduced to 24 finalists who will arrive on Mars sequentially in six groups of four.

Can you believe this? People with impressive credentials, spanning a variety of age groups and nationalities are ready and willing to meet and face <u>the challenge of their curiosity</u> even when we have no conclusive data showing the possibility of human survival – can you imagine this? A one-way trip to Mars – approximately 50 million miles away from the place we all share space and call home. I hear you muttering there is no place like home. I agree! Yet our curiosity driven questions keep driving us to ask the question <u>why</u> and <u>why not</u>? For those Mars finalists – they ask why not me? Some challenge isn't? Think we should spend a bit of our Question Wonderland time kicking around some examples of our curiosity questioning instincts. We should not be surprised to find that evidences of human curiosity take us back long before JOB's time and bring us to our present time as we speak.

Let's gather our thoughts, and then we can kick around a couple of curiosity questioning examples while moving right along.

CHAPTER 6

WHAT'S THAT STRANGE FIRE?

Why does it keep burning?

I am sure that both of us, if we try really hard, we can recall seeing something that cannot be explained and did not seem possible. I remember as a boy I liked watching magical "stunts" performed by famous magicians. I was puzzled then and even now as I think back, I still haven't figured out whether I saw what I saw or did those magicians do what they did. Is that why they call it magic?

Every civilization produced their share of magicians. The earlier cultures that populated the Fertile Crescent – the middle and near east – were steeped in these mystic shenanigans. For example, the Egyptians and the Babylonians for generations practiced the magic arts that were so real and so feared that even their kings and rulers were in awe of their mystic power. To play it safe these rulers like the Pharaoh and Abimelech consulted them and did everything to keep them happy. The gesture of placating these magicians was like "hush money" for avoiding "unnatural mischiefs" that could result.

Did you know that Egyptian magicians could, and showed that they could, turn a wooden rod into a serpent? How could that be? Great question?

Ever heard of a man named Moses? In World Literature we read about Moses as the great lawgiver and a legendary leader of the Jewish people, leading the ancient Jews out of Egypt toward the promised land of Palestine. Moses attracts and rivets our attention because of the spectacular episodes of his life.

From his birth and infancy when his mother prepared a device that doubled as an infant's crib and a lifeboat, to the drama that framed his whole life. When he was only three months old, prevailing circumstances threatening his life were aborted by the "lifeboat" that helped save him from being a casualty of the Egyptian Pharaoh's order to kill all Jewish boys at birth. Moses miraculously survived – not by magic but by mystery of what the Bible calls Omnipotent Mystery. The Bible story in Exodus, starting at chapter one gives a detailed account of his life from the time of his rescue, his period of nurturing by his mother, his upbringing in the palace of the Pharaoh and subsequent experiences in his storied exemplary life.

I see you are showing real interest in the excerpts of Moses' life. I am not sure why, may be you can share your thoughts during our next break. For me just talking with you about Moses inspires me, so I want to be careful to stay on our point about the innate curiosity driving our questions. What is my point you say? Here is my point. I am amazed at the similarities in the human experience and the similarities in our innate curiosity as we trace back <u>thousands of years</u> in the history of our siblings.

Where is the Moses similarity? Here it comes! First his up and downs and ups and down again – then finally up! Moses was <u>up</u>, when rescued out of the Nile River in his "lifeboat". Moses was <u>up</u>, when given "contracted" caretaking and nurturing by his own mother. Moses was <u>up</u>, during his life in the Egyptian palace as a Prince of Egypt. Moses went <u>down</u>, when he fled to Midian to avoid the heavy hand of Egyptian justice for avenging the murder of one of his Jewish brothers. He spent forty years in Midian as a shepherd. A steep plunge – from Egyptian Prince – in line to rule Egypt - to a shepherd not even owning the sheep he cared for. That's how <u>far down Moses plunged</u>. He was now eighty years old that's how far along he had travelled in time. That's as far as similarities go for most of us – I think. Don't hold our breath! Look at this moment in Moses' up and down experiences and watch for at <u>least one similarity</u>: <u>curiosity and the question</u> it generated. <u>Why does this bush keep burning</u>? What bush is that you ask? Here comes the Bible again to give us insight into

41

this questioning curiosity factor common to all of us. In the
third chapter of Exodus, let's look at this together:

> *"Now Moses was tending the flock of Jethro his father-
> in-law, the priest of Midian, and he led the flock to
> the far side of the wilderness and came to Horeb,
> the mountain of God. ² There the angel of the Lord
> appeared to him in flames of fire from within a bush.
> Moses saw that though the bush was on fire it did not
> burn up. ³ So Moses thought, "I will go over and see
> this strange sight—why the bush does not burn up."*
> *⁴ When the Lord saw that he had gone over to look,
> God called to him from within the bush, "Moses!
> Moses!" And Moses said, "Here I am."*
> *⁵ "Do not come any closer," God said. "Take off your
> sandals, for the place where you are standing is holy
> ground." ⁶ Then he said, "I am the God of your father,
> the God of Abraham, the God of Isaac and the God of
> Jacob." At this, Moses hid his face, because he was
> afraid to look at God.*
> *⁷ The Lord said, "I have indeed seen the misery of
> my people in Egypt. I have heard them crying out
> because of their slave drivers, and I am concerned
> about their suffering. ⁸ So I have come down to rescue
> them from the hand of the Egyptians and to bring them
> up out of that land into a good and spacious land, a
> land flowing with milk and honey—the home of the*

Canaanites, Hittites, Amorites, Perizzites, Hivites and Jebusites.⁹ And now the cry of the Israelites has reached me, and I have seen the way the Egyptians are oppressing them. ¹⁰ So now, go. I am sending you to Pharaoh to bring my people the Israelites out of Egypt."

¹¹ But Moses said to God, "Who am I that I should go to Pharaoh and bring the Israelites out of Egypt?" ¹² And God said, "I will be with you. And this will be the sign to you that it is I who have sent you: When you have brought the people out of Egypt, you[b] will worship God on this mountain." (Ex. 3:1-12)

Remember the ups and downs of Moses' life? He is now in a <u>down moment of time and place</u> in his eighty years of life – so it seems! He is caring for sheep (his father-in-law's flock) and his eyes caught the sight of a burning bush. If you have been in or near the Sinai area in the summertime you should have no problem understanding the sight of a burning bush. In these areas temperatures can creep up to 120°F in the shade. So bushes can catch fire without any "magic." This sight of a burning bush would perhaps have been unnoticed by some of us, <u>but not Moses</u>! Moses was brimming with Curiosity! Instead of moving around in his shepherding routine, he **turned aside** to see **why the bush** that was burning, **just kept burning.** In other words – no ashes, just non-stop burning of this strange bush! In our words, we would say

– his curiosity got the best of him! Has this ever been your experience? Well, it's been mine, more than once.

Notice this from our Scripture reading that it was when the Lord saw that Moses' curiosity prompted him from a casual observation to raise the question (paraphrased): "why is this bush still burning non-stop," that Moses was cautioned not to draw near, but to remove his shoes because the presence of an Omnipotent God, requires and deserves utmost respect and total adoration. What are we learning from this classic narrative of ancient Biblical Literature? You say that you would like my thoughts? Ok, can't wait to say that my first lesson is the affirmation of my faith is rock solid! What do you mean by that statement you ask? There is a popular notion that man evolved from some lower form of living organism to what he has become. It really should be what he is becoming. If you look carefully in the archives of his history you will find that long, long, before Moses there was Adam the first created being. You will also notice that while he understood the latitude he had to eat any and all the "fruit" within his reach, he seemed not to resist taking and eating the one fruit that was forbidden. He had not tasted it until Eve offered it to him. He could have refused! Why didn't he? He was CURIOUS! He asked himself – why not try it, I may like it. You know the rest of the story.

Curiosity and its associated questions are intrinsic to our human nature. It is at the core of human progress. It can lead us toward the path of destruction and separation from our

Creator, as in the case of Adam. It can also be the starting point of something bigger than ourselves, as in the case of Moses. Please notice in the trajectory of Moses' life – if there were no curiosity question at the burning bush, there would be no assignment to lead the "children of Israel" out of Egypt. There would be no miraculous crossing of the Red Sea. Not by Moses to be sure!

Curiosity whether exhibited by Adam or Moses is unique to the human species because of the rational questions it generates. Did you realize that curiosity is what made you join me on this Question Wonderland trip? Perhaps the question you asked, why should I make this trip with someone I don't know or never met. Like Moses at the Burning Bush, you may not think that this is a critical juncture in your life's journey. Perhaps it is in this Question Wonderland that you will hear the voice of God from the burning bush of our conversation.

It may be that as you consider the ups and downs of Moses' life, you find that you may be at a <u>down</u> moment in your life but God could be speaking to you through this conversation. You may remember that one of the greatest miracles involving any human being – involved Moses! Remember the Burning Bush that got his curiosity and attention and his question – what is that strange bush burning on and on? No Burning Bush – no Red Sea Miracle! My friend, my burning bush encounter was when I heard the Voice of God by the reading of His Word and accepting the Lord Jesus as my Savior. I experienced the miracle of eternal life and peace with the God of Adam and Moses by the reading of His Word, accepting, and following its instructions. Among these Scriptures is the one I leave for your reference and action step:

> *"For God so loved the world that he gave his one and only Son, that whoever believes in him shall not perish but have eternal life." John 3:16*

You say you are up for another example of curiosity question.

Ok, let's roll!

CHAPTER 7

ARE WE ALONE IN THE UNIVERSE?

Is any one out there?

The more we hop from topic to topic in our Wonderland conversation, the more insight we are sharing about the unique curiosity factor that is common to all of us siblings, descendants of Adam and Eve.

It seems that the inherited curiosity DNA imbedded in our forbears from creation remained constant throughout all the generations of history, including our own, except for one caveat. What's the caveat, you ask? I think there has been a paradigm shift in the worldview of a created universe versus one that resulted from the fragments of a "Big Bang." The regrettable paradigm shift is a progressive movement away from the Bible as our guide for <u>information</u> and <u>instruction</u>

about all things, all people, and all places in the universe and for all times.

To get a flavor for the incredible speed of this shift in our curiosity thinking, consider that until 1961 any discussion about living beings, (extraterrestrial life) among the stars, in other words, and the possibility of life, like ours among other planets, was the sole territory of science fiction. Fact is, it was taboo in social conversations. No one can precisely nail down just when science fiction thinking morphed into the collective thinking of the science and technology community. Slowly but surely there is developing a curiosity obsession among a rare breed of scientists – SETI – the acronym for Search for Extraterrestrial Intelligence. You are asking if there is any reason to give any credulity to the people of science who literally work round the clock on shifts motivated by this curiosity question? They go to sleep and wake up in the morning with this question: "Are we alone in the universe?"

The question you raise is a good one. My response is simple, with two "ifs." If you are a completely secular person with no acceptance of the Good Book – the Bible as the first and last words about the universe and its function, you will have no problem with the curiosity obsession that drives the question we are discussing: "Are we alone in the universe?" Let me hasten to say, your puzzling questions about life beyond the stars, are not unique. Your view is shared by many and increasingly so. On the other hand, if you accept the Scriptures as the ultimate source of information about the universe, then you might find the current scientific "stampede" to pick up radio signals from living beings on planets millions of light years away, really futile. The beautiful thing about our conversation is that it preserves the respect for each other's views without critique or confrontation. Isn't that great?

Let's take a brief look at the two (2) views aimed at the question: Are we alone in the universe? Is any one out there? Let's take the "secular" view first (Bible aside). It's reasonable to think that during the last two (2) centuries our civilization has progressed remarkably in most areas of our survival activity. There are admittedly some essential areas where we need to clean up our act, but we can consider those challenge driven questions later. For simplicity, let's brief the secular worldview on the curious question of – Who is out there? and What are they doing? We want to know. Why not persist given our advanced equipment and resources. We have technology that not so long ago was the fodder of science fiction and the elements of wild imagination.

Remember Star Wars, remember Stephen Spielberg's movie in 1982, dramatizing E. T. from outer space? That movie made believers out of many who watched as Elliot – the lonely little boy who befriended a stranded E. T. who found his way to earth only to find a very strange environment. Then better yet, remember those years in the early sixties when the media kept us busy with news breakers about flying saucers, and little green men cited in some areas of the country? As I recall they didn't appear in New York or New Jersey. Perhaps – too many people moving like crazy during the days and too many dazzling lights at night in the cities.

If you remember, it really got us thinking that – you know what, there could be some people like ourselves out there somewhere. If we keep pressing our curiosity question buttons we may find that E. T. really landed here because he lost his way. This is not an easy topic or an easy question to answer, depending on your bent or perspective.

What's my world view you ask? My worldview is very simple. That's because I am a simple person with a grateful attitude. What do I mean? First I am grateful to God for the blessing of a sound mind. For example, it is with that simple mind of mine that got me thinking like JOB (remember him), when he looked up to the starry heavens and maybe considered – Any one out there like me? Is there life among the stars? You say did JOB ask that question? He sure did – that's from the Bible: let's read it here:

"Can you by searching find out God? Can you find out the Almighty unto perfection?" Job 11:7

My interpretation of those sage words of Scripture guides my thinking and all the curiosity questions that pop up in my mind about maters on earth or in the universe of stars and planets above us. So what is my <u>bottom line</u> answer to the question: Are we alone in the universe? Is anyone out there?

I gave my bottom line answer and as a bonus, I'll brief you on what supports that bottom line answer.

First, I totally and unequivocally accept the Holy Scripture as God's inspired Word. I accept and believe that it covers all, with no exception, questions conceived or imagined by the mind of man. I accept and believe that God created the universe including this terrestrial ball we call earth! I also believe that if there were any other created beings like ourselves anywhere else out there among the galaxy of stars and planets – we would be informed as we are about all other aspects of our existence. Scripture never even hinted at any E. T. beings on any planet.

By my FAITH, I have revamped any "secular" thinking or imagining about E. T. and firmly believe that the world, the universe – was formed by God.

"By faith we understand that the universe was formed
at God's command, so that what is seen was not made
out of what was visible." Heb. 11:3

My FAITH also allows me to conclude that if we are not alone on this planet earth, somewhere in Scripture we would find that information. My FAITH also allows me to conclude that if there were a "Big Bang" that resulted in the mysterious universe, that spectacular event would be recorded in the Scripture. My friend, I mention this faith factor because it is so essential in addressing the "far out" curiosity question:

Who is out there? Faith can, and does creep into every crevice of our thinking and curiosity questioning.

Occasionally I sit in reflection on some of my mentally rigorous experiences during my engineering training at the City College of New York. I think back on some of the requirements imposed on us students. Some of them we thought were unnecessary. Some of them seemed impossible. I thought of some mathematical proofs that were really an exercise in mental discipline. You miss a step and the whole exercise falls apart and you prove nothing! Guess what? Before starting some of these proofs which we later needed for (in math lingo) derivations of more difficult solutions we had to make statements of: assumptions! Without these assumptions –"simplifying assumptions" – you can solve none of these seemingly impossible problems.

I am so glad you are asking – what were these assumptions? Are you ready for this? They were statements of FAITH! These were principles which we applied to the exercise which were believed (assumed) based on previous math and physics text material. That, I confess, was one of the eye-openers regarding the power of faith. Even in searching out the most complex problems or answering the most "far out" questions – like are we alone in the universe? My faith allows me the confidence to share with you that faith, simple faith, provides the only way to get answers about the mysterious heavens. What's out there, and who is out there. Faith can escort you to some surprising details.

If you believe the Scriptures, you will discover, that the God who created the universe we discussed earlier, is the same God who gives us His word in (1 Cor. 2:9) regarding those who have placed FAITH in His Son – Jesus Christ. These words are – let's look at the verse in 1 Cor. 2:9 together:

> *"However, as it is written: what no eye has seen, what no ear has heard, and what no human mind has conceived"* the things God has prepared for those who love him."

If we took the secular route in answering the question: <u>Are we alone in the</u> <u>Universe</u>? <u>Is anyone out there</u>? We would be on this topic for endless days. But if we are on the same page or pages – the Bible pages – Eureka! We got the answer! now we are all set to move to questions of challenges.

PART 2

QUESTIONS DRIVEN BY CHALLENGES

CHAPTER 8

CHALLENGE OF THE SKIES

The sky is no limit

We have been kicking around the very interesting topic of curiosity-prompted questions, i.e. questions that our curiosity will not restrain us from asking. What do you say? I agree with you completely when you say that we haven't even skimmed the surface of those types of questions. You say, what about a few questions that are triggered by challenge? Ok we can tackle that if you like.

Before we take a rest break and regroup our thoughts to engage another area of interesting questions, let's take a quick look at how intrepid our generation of curiosity non-stop questions keep pushing the boundaries of questions.

Remember our discussion on the 'ambitious' plan to land humans on Mars by 2024? Ready for this: National Aeronautics Space Administration (NASA) has a New

Frontier Program that has been focusing on the planet Jupiter because of its suspected potential for human life support. So you thought Mars was or is a 'way out' challenge?

You may recall that in 1995, NASA launched its first space expedition to Jupiter. The satellite spacecraft Galileo performed over twelve close-up flybys of Europa. No! No! Not Eureka – Europa. This is a satellite of the planet Jupiter and is one of its sixty moons with suspected potential support for life exploration. Now listen to this, from data sent back to earth by Galileo, NASA's team spent twelve years sorting out the data. They 'suspect' that Europa has within its structure liquid water and the necessary chemistry: (i.e. oxygen and nitrogen) that is required for human life support.

Now check this out for a real stretch of Challenge Questions. We are not even close to landing humans on Mars – approximately 150 million miles from earth, but we are challenged by what we imagine to be going on up there on Europa, 500 million miles away approximately – 350 million miles further away than Mars and requiring about six years of travel to reach. The challenge? Why can't we do the impossible? By the way, did you ever ask this question; where did this indomitable nature of mankind and his persistent and probing instinct to confront all challenge come from? Where did all these questions originate?

Remember earlier on, when we entered Question Wonderland I mentioned that my handy reference (The Holy Bible) in my backpack has answers to all questions that the mind of man can ever conceive? Let's see if that's a valid statement. Let's look together here in the book of Genesis, Chapter 11: 1-9

"Now the whole world had one language and a common speech. As men moved eastward, they found a plain in Shinar and settled there. They said to each other, "Come, let's make bricks and bake them thoroughly." They used brick instead of stone, and tar for mortar. Then they said, "Come, let us build ourselves a city, with a tower that reaches to the heavens, so that we may make a name for ourselves and not be scattered over the face of the whole earth." But the LORD came down to see the city and the tower that the men were building. The LORD said, "If as one people speaking the same language they have begun to do this, then nothing they plan to do will be impossible for them. Come, let us go down and confuse their language so they will not understand each other." So the LORD scattered them from there over all the earth, and they stopped building the city. That is why it was called Babel--because there the LORD confused the language of the whole world. From there the LORD scattered them over the face of the whole earth."

Verse 4 says that these earlier settlers, our ancestors, primitive as they were <u>with limited equipment and limited resources</u>, were not limited by their obsession to confront challenges.

You ask me how do I get that idea out of these verses we read together? Well, just think with me for a second. These primitive people (offspring of God's creation) had no knowledge of the concept of gravity. They somehow knew how to mix mortar and make bricks. They looked around and were curious as they gazed up to the heavens above with no idea about how far into distance they were gazing.

Look at the enormous challenge they faced. Here is what should amaze us – they said: why can't we reach up to these high heavens? Let's build a city, and let's build a tower to reach into the heavens so that we will leave our mark on our civilization and questions to be answered by the next generation. Look at the soundness in the sequence of their logical thought and logical steps that they considered and executed. One day, someone woke up and asked the question: why should we be baffled by the vast distance of the heavens? Why should we be restrained by the mystery of the dazzling heavenly lights? Let's stop asking <u>why</u> and ask <u>why not</u> build a tower that will reach up and explore the heavens. If God is up there we will find Him. Ever heard of the Babel Tower? Our handy reference in (Genesis 11:8) shows that before these sky gazers and tower builders got very far and before the ill-conceived structure was erected the project was aborted. These, our ancestors, could never know that their descendants, our generation separated by thousands of years, would progress intrepid questions of challenge to the point that there seems no heights that we cannot reach and no mystery we cannot solve.

In this, our generation, we have new toolboxes of techno-gadgets and digital devices that give rapid responses to the seeming impossible questions we keep asking. There are no limits to our appetite to face down and overcome challenges. There are no boundaries to our questions. Ours is a generation of aggressive questioners. Something, somewhere within the human spirit, somewhere in our genes, in our makeup there is a never-ending drive never to be deterred by any challenge despite all evidence of seeming impossibility. Is this a good thing you ask? I think it is! I know it is. It is a God given implant, endowment, and enablement. You and I may share pleasant surprises if you wish to kick around some of these unique God-given characteristics that you and I and our fellow mortals share.

After we digest some of these eye-opening thoughts we have been sharing about challenge-driven questions we will slow down a bit to take in some of the serenity and natural flavor of this peaceful **wonderland of questions**. Isn't it neat that we don't have to hurry to catch the next train or bus, or arrive at the workplace at a given time? Isn't it a blessing to make this unhurried trip together? You say you forgot that they ever made a smart-phone, I-pad or I-phone. Same here. Speaking of smart devices I am sure you have some smart ideas on challenge-type questions.

CHAPTER 9

DIFFERENT STROKES FOR DIFFERENT FOLKS

Some run with the bulls and some walk with sheep

It's interesting how expressions pop up and then they fade away as time passes. There are those expressions that seem to hang around for a long time. How about this one – "Different strokes for different folks" – remember that one? Let's kick around some challenge-type questions that are different because the folks who ask these questions are very different. You pick a few and I'll pick a few. You say your questions will be random. That's ok! That's what this wonderland stroll is all about. It's about a delightful ambiance for insightful and interesting conversation.

That's a great question you just asked. It's really a priority question. Let me make sure I get it straight. You are asking why do some of our 'fellow persons' see challenges – obstacles, impossibilities, etc. – and they not only ask why, they ask why not, and many <u>BRAVE</u> souls ask <u>why not me</u>? Are you saying – you think these dare-devil types like Nick Wallenda of Niagara Falls fame, who ask these challenge-driven questions are just plain crazy or recklessly looking for fame or fortune – perhaps both? They seem to have no personal regard for the sanctity of their own lives or how the grief and discomfort that their reckless 'adventure' may affect family and friends.

You know, my friend, I agree with you on the crazy-daredevil description of their questions, but I think if we look a little closer and at the right source of information we may get a hint or clue to what passes for bravery, courage and supernatural confidence in confronting challenge.

Do you recall earlier on, I mentioned that, as we keep discussing questions, JOB of Bible times, will give us a lot of help? Thousands of years ago JOB in his extreme series of dilemmas, wished he was never born. His suffering was so shattering that, he raised a question that has puzzled the human mind for ages and ages.

Somewhere, all of us at some time come to grips with thoughts about God. God, who is not like us – visible to our eyes. The old hymn I remember gives the hint of God – <u>all wise, immortal, invisible</u> and truly <u>incomprehensible</u>, but very much in touch with us at all times whether we believe it, or like it, or not.

Yet listen to JOB's question: Talk about a challenge driven question – here it comes from the Book of JOB Chapter 11:7. Let's read it right here from our handy Bible:

"Can you fathom the mysteries of God?   Can you probe the limits of the Almighty?"

You ask where do I find challenge in JOB's question? Well, think back on the very brief discussion we had about the immensity and complexity of the heavens above us that we call the universe of space. Think of a Creator who started it all and keeps it maintained and who chooses to be invisible to the human eyes. One exception! What's that? The story line in the greatest story ever told is that the Great Creator became our Savior and all God's fullness was met in Him. The Gospel of John in the New Testament said it best: John Chapter 1:18

"No man hath seen God at any time, the only begotten Son, which is in the bosom of the Father, he hath declared him".

That should be of great comfort to JOB – that's the answer to his question really. You might say his question was a bit premature! His question was nonetheless, full of challenge. His challenge – to find God! Can I really search and find our invisible God? Can I find Him even if I am able to conduct a perfect search for that perfect one? JOB was not crazy! He was totally INSPIRED, as we will see later.

For now, to your point about why people ask these challenge-driven questions: My thoughts are these: these people, you and I to some extent included, represent the reality of our human experience. Some of us do not want to hear about challenge, some of us do not want to be within a hair's breadth of challenge, and some of us see challenge and quickly rush to the exit. On the other hand there are those of us, by our nature are polar opposites. The greater the challenge the greater the passion in the question: why, why not, why not me? So there is variety for you!

If you think they are not patterns in God's creation: look at the races of human beings – same origin, but look at the variety in racial appearances. Look at the flowers of the fields, what an array of dazzling beauty – this is exquisite variety at its best. This is the <u>Mystery of Man</u>! And to your point – <u>the mystery of his ever questioning mind</u>. Better yet you realize the mystery of his Creator!

There in this inquisitive nature of our 'fellow persons' are the traits that prompt their never ending urge to question challenge. They have an unbelievable disregard for any fear of failure; or any consequence of death; or any lack of compensation for their daring accomplishments. They dismiss criticism from incredulous spectators who insist they need to have some kind of sober advice and counsel. You say, that you have 'different' words for those crazy types?

Strange as it may seem, I really haven't answered your question as to why these challenge-driven questions drive our passionate 'neighbors' to face off these seemingly crazy-dare-devil adventures. Just in case I don't get back on this point, here is a thought you may want to consider! The drive to confront challenge with the why, why not questions, did not originate with us. Oh! You say! My friend, I said exactly that. You see, here again, the Good Book comes to our rescue!

In Genesis Chapter 1:2 we read that the Great Creator created 'Man' and empowered him to have dominion over every 'living' thing on the earth. In his pristine innocent state – no challenge was beyond his reach – All dominion was his commission! Your eyes are popping wider as we look this over in our handy reference. What happened you say? Well, our ancestors lost it (their dominion) when they disobeyed the clear instructions of God.

Why can't our fellow mortals pull off some of those impossible feats they ask questions about? Don't know? Well, I know, the One who said these words – "Without me you can do nothing." I believe these words! (John 15:5). Without Him we wouldn't be having this conversation about challenge-driven questions. My simple comment to your earlier question: crazy as some of these 'outside-the-box' challenge questions may seem - only by God's enablement can these challenge-driven questions be answered in the affirmative. Well, we will move right along to some other interesting questions. Let's try one that resonates with all of us because it received such wide and sustained publicity worldwide. By the way, did you ever run with the Bulls in Spain? How about watching the shepherds mind their sheep on the suburbs of Jerusalem? If you have, what do you think of the running with the bulls versus shepherding sheep? Just a bit of trivia to lighten up the conversation about "different strokes for different folks" before we move on.

CHAPTER 10

THE RODNEY KING QUESTION

Ever heard of Rodney King?

H ere is a tricky question for you. It's tricky because it does not seem to have challenge written all over it but if you look closer you can't miss the challenge at the center of it. Can I give you a hint you say? Sure I can. Think back to the Los Angeles, USA riots of 1992. Think of what triggered that violent outrage causing destruction of life and property in a city renowned for entertaining the world.

Think of the non-stop media coverage of Los Angeles police beating, battering and bashing of the 27-year old construction worker who was alleged to be driving under the influence of alcohol. Think of how the nation held its breath as they witnessed a mini television version of the civil rights earthquakes that shook the nation to its deepest core less than four decades earlier.

Does the name Rodney King ring a bell? Yeah, yeah so you say so reminiscently! Yes Rodney King! He is the one. His likeness remains in my memory. That grisly scene is stored in my mental file that stores remote pictures of the past. If you recall, after the brutal beating episode and the media frenzy subsided, Rodney King seemed to have disappeared for a while. Some of us were reminded of that well-known Bible parable of the Good Samaritan. We thought of Rodney in that 'half dead' condition, as was the case of the man in the parable who fell among thieves as he took that ill-fated journey from Jerusalem to Jericho. Rodney King in fact may have been more than half dead. Rodney fell among merciless Los Angeles cops.

Another fact is, he was almost brain dead and not expected to make it. But miracle of miracles – Rodney survived and a while later <u>emerged with a question</u>! Remember his question? Don't sweat it if you forgot his exact words. They were simple words but searching, sensitive and sage!

Here was his question: <u>CAN WE ALL GET ALONG</u>? This question deserves pause for a moment of thought so we can connect the question to the challenge that prompted it.

It would surprise me very much if the Nobel Nominating Committee in Oslo, Norway thought of asking my opinion for setting up a category for awarding **the most profound question in human relations in our time – perhaps of all time.** If that should ever happen (not a chance) my immediate submission would be – without the blink of an eye – Rodney King's question - <u>CAN WE ALL GET ALONG</u>?

If you think of my vote for Rodney's Nobel nomination as a capricious gesture let me explain. It seems the answer could be: of course we can all get along! The follow-up question then would be – why not? Well that's the rub – why not? What do you say to that 'why not' question? You are stuck? Well we have never failed to be rescued if and when we are stuck for an answer to any question of any kind. We reach for and into our <u>source book The Holy Bible.</u> Are you ok with that statement?

How far back should we go to take a brief look into – why? Can we all get along? And really the question purports that we are not getting along. That's a given. Just listen to the news and watch television or Google the Internet. So why not? Let's look at the closest we can get to the origin of this social challenge. God the creator made this master-piece – man the paragon of the species – humankind. Back in Genesis chapter 2 we read after Adam and Eve degraded their perfection and innocence by their disobedience to God's clear and specific command, they were dismissed from the pristine paradise which was designed for their life and living. They had reproductive capacity. In other words they, (Adam and Eve), (Genesis Chapter 4) had at first two sons – Cain and Abel. You are gleaming! (remember the Bible story from where? Church/Sunday School or whatever). Well, let me take you to the earliest challenge these two brothers faced! What was that you ask?

Let's see if you agree (here in Genesis Chapter 4:2) we read that the two brothers chose different career paths: Cain went for farming –agriculture; Abel went for ranching – cattle rearing. At this point the Bible does not give us the details regarding their instructions about the offering they should present in worship to God and also how it should be done. What we do know is that these were blood brothers, closer they could not be. I mean real brothers. They seem to have been <u>getting</u> <u>along</u> very well until 'offering time' came around. Cain's offering taken from his farm was refused by God. (Genesis 4:3-5)

> *"In the course of time Cain brought some of the fruits of the soil as an offering to the Lord. And Abel also brought an offering—fat portions from some of the firstborn of his flock. The Lord looked with favor on Abel and his offering, but on Cain and his offering he did not look with favor. So Cain was very angry, and his face was downcast."*

Abel brought his offering from his ranch – his offering was accepted.

Now listen or look closely at these verses: Cain did not get mad when his offering was rejected, but when Abel's offering was accepted then he really got hopping mad (Genesis 4:6-7).

Let's simplify the words that God spoke to Cain: "Why are you so mad that your rage is showing all over you. You were told what to do <u>but</u> <u>you</u> <u>chose</u> <u>what</u> <u>you</u> <u>wanted</u> <u>to</u> <u>do</u>." The next thing we see is that Cain went looking for his brother and murdered him in cold blood!

Now here is where we need to take a few steps back and look at the challenge that these two brothers faced in getting along. If we further simplify what we have read: we see that the challenge for Cain was this: Yes I know what I should do, <u>but</u> why not bring an offering to God that I think should be ok? In other words – why do I have to obey God? When God responded by rejecting Cain's offering – he could not aim his anger at God (the Creator) so he displaced his furious aggressive anger in the murder of his brother! That was the end of 'getting along'.

Talk about the importance of questions. Listen (Genesis 4:9) to the question from God to Cain? "Where is Abel your brother?" Think that God, who is all knowing, did not know where Able was? Listen to Cain's answer: "<u>I</u> <u>know</u> <u>not</u>! <u>Am</u> <u>I</u> <u>my</u> <u>brother's</u> <u>keeper</u>?" Wait a minute, let's get our heads together or better yet, our thoughts together and think about Cain's response. First thought – what was Cain's view of God if he thought God did not know that he murdered his brother? You munch on that question. You seem eager to get to the real question!

You know what, I don't blame you at all for your eagerness to grapple with Cain's question: "**Am I my brother's**

keeper?" My friend, isn't it clearer than crystal that after the passing of thousands of years, today as we are speaking and casually strolling through this imaginary Question Wonderland, there are but a precious few of our fellow human beings who understand the social and spiritual importance and impact of Cain's question and how it connects with Rodney King's question: "**Can we all get along?**" Getting along in peace and harmony is not an impossible challenge. It's admittedly a difficult challenge that raises the deeper question. **Are we our brother's keeper?**

Let me press your memory button again. Remember the name John Donne? Yes or no. He was this 17th century English lawyer/poet who became famous not only for his legal prowess, but for his classic poem titled "**No man is an island.**" I recall an excerpt from his poem:

> "*No man is an island, entire of itself, every one is a part of the continent, everyone is part of the main, everyone's death diminishes me because I am involved in mankind, and therefore never send to know for whom the bells toll, it tolls for thee.*"

Do you realize that John Donne who penned those memorable words, and you, and I, and all our fellow mortals share a common ancestral linkage to that fellow in the Bible we were discussing – yes, we are all connected to Cain who asked "**Am I my brother's keeper?**"

Really, I think we may have the key to connect the linkage between the challenge questions raised by two human beings Cain of the Bible and Rodney King of the 1992 Los Angeles police brutality event thousands of years apart. Really, if we get the sense of John Donne's poem (which he may have taken from Bible readings) that is: "we are our brother's keeper." We are a fellowship of mortals – male and female – we are fellows in the same ship of a common humanity. Also, guess what, we can connect that link to Rodney's question – "Can we all get along?" Yes we can all get along if and only if we become and remain aware that we are, every single one of us, dependent on each other's love, nurture, care, concern and support.

Do you think there is a simple answer to the question of why we can all get along? These instructions are clearly stated in the New Testament section of the Bible. Here are two references: Phil. 2:4 and Gal.6:10

"*Not looking to your own interests but each of you to the interests of the others.*"

"*Therefore, as we have opportunity, let us do good to all people, especially to those who belong to the family of believers.*"

You can look at them when we take our rest break. I can see from the quizzical look on your face that you think we have created a real quandary for ourselves by recalling questions that press against the greatest social challenge of all the ages: **Am I my brother's keeper?** – Can we all get along? These questions will not leave our thoughts even if we wish them away.

As for answers, that's another story. You smile? I smile with you because I really believe the answer is inscribed in the greatest story ever told. If you wish we can pick this up later after our break. I am sorry, did you say, you would like to hear more about how those challenge questions apply to our world view in our post-modern world of now? Well, let's catch our breath and we will pick it up in a few.

CHAPTER 11

THE QUESTION OF THE HORSE AND THE CART

Which comes first?

I t does not surprise me at all that you want to continue talking through the questions we have been discussing about the two brothers (Cain and Abel and Rodney King), separated in time not by centuries but thousands of years of social progress.

Since you want us to further kick around some thoughts that connect Cain's question – "Am I my brother's keeper?" to Rodney King's question – "Can we all get along?" Let's see which question comes first as a link in our chain of thought. You say – obviously, the horse comes first because the cart will go nowhere without the pull or power of the horse.

This takes us first to the point of Cain's question – a classic social challenge: each of us, fellow mortals, and descendants from the same ancestors, is endowed with responsibility to be loving, caring, nurturing, and compassionate to each other as 'brothers' aka fellow human beings. Talk about questions! We have to keep reminding ourselves that questions! – questions! That's what this Wonderland is all about.

So from our earlier conversation, why do you think Cain responded to the question about his brother's presence by asking the infamous question: "Am I my brother's keeper?" You have no idea you say? Well my thoughts are based on the Scriptures we read earlier in Genesis Chapter 4.

If you recall, Abel came to worship God and presented his offering from the first born of his flocks. This offering was what God required, and it was accepted. Are we ok so far on the recall? Now, Cain did not get mad when God accepted his younger brother Abel's offering. He got really mad when he brought his offering and was rejected, because he decided to present an offering of worship following the script of his own making – in other words I'll do it my way!

The question from Cain: "Am I my brother's keeper?" is a question from the ages past, but that is the question we must first cover before we tackle the question "Can we all get along?" On a very positive note, I am so very thankful to God that there are many (really far too few) who have a sense that no person is an island; entire of itself every person is a part of the continent, a part of a common geography. Everyone has a social responsibility to the other without any consideration of racial or ethnic origins. There are those who don't make the news but they sincerely embrace this credo.

I am my brother's keeper! That's the challenge to all those who side with Cain in asking the question in the converse. How do I connect all these questions that present us with the most unsettling and perplexing problems of our post-modern world. How you ask? Do you remember 9/11/2001? Everyone, almost everywhere in the world catches an ominous pause when recalling that horrific event that snuffed out the lives of over 3,000 people from many countries including the majority from New York City. It was no secret that this tragic event was carefully planned under the Islam label of Jihad. We all watched the video shown of Osama Ben Laden's rejoicing over the violent assault on the World Trade Center Twin Towers. This was a savage assault against innocent victims in the name of Jihad – a holy war against the 'infidels'!

Ben Laden's Jihad, which during the same day, attacked the United States in New York, Pennsylvania and Washington D.C., was evidence of a complete refusal to accept the responsibility (challenge) intended for all us earth dwellers. The Jihad group is infuriated – real mad (like Cain) because non-Muslims do not worship as they do. Fact is they see this whole population of non-Muslims as infidels - another term for devils. We are not their brothers because we do not worship as they do. Remember Cain and Abel? They were brothers, but they worshipped differently. For this Abel was murdered.

The new ISIS threat worldwide that was kicked off recently is a continuation of the Jihad concept of eliminating those who do not worship as they do. Do you notice from our reading together of the Scripture in Genesis Chapter 4 that Cain launched a one-man Jihad against his younger brother? Why? Because Abel's worship was different than his and Abel's was accepted by God while his was rejected.

While this rage in the hearts of some of our fellowmen still prevails we can only hope and continue to pray that the Bible message of peace and harmony (the Gospel) will reach the hearts of those who do not see their fellowmen as human neighbors or brothers/sisters sharing space on this globe we call planet earth.

By the way, as you reflect on these timeless and timely questions, remember that despite the genius of our brains and the accomplishments of our efforts we must, as a people, turn Cain's question into a reversed statement: We are our brother's keeper. To the point of Rodney King's question! My thought is: why can't we embrace as a personal credo: that we are our brother's keeper? To that extent we may move toward the answer to the question – can we all get along?

You know what? A thought just popped into my head! I thought of how unique the Bible is. It connects so precisely things past and present and makes so clear what we all need to know and practice in our everyday lives. Would you believe that there is a verse in the New Testament that speaks specifically and directly to what we are discussing regarding Cain and Abel. Is that in the Bible you ask? Here let me read it with you (Hebrews 11:4) it says:

"By faith Abel offered to God a better sacrifice than Cain did. By faith he was commended as a righteous man where God spoke well of his offerings, and by faith he still speaks, even though he is dead."

We can try, and we should keep trying to heed the words of the ancient prophet Amos. God has shown us what he requires of us:

"To do justly, show mercy and to walk humbly with our God."

So do we have the horse before the cart?

History has shown that we have failed miserably in putting the horse and the cart in their proper harness. My friend, I share these thoughts with you from a full heart, full of thanks to God that in his salvation plan of love and grace he has made the seemingly impossible human challenge possible. He developed a master plan, to change our hearts, from which spring murders, violence, and all kinds of disruptive acts like those that chill our spine as we watch, read and hear daily media reports.

Here is a question, I am sure you have asked privately, why do so many people like: Doctors Without Borders, Mercy Ships, Samaritan Purse, World Vision, Red Cross, Salvation Army, Operation Mobilization, America's Keswick and Recovery Center, Food For The Poor, CARE, Voice of the Martyr's, Christian Mission in Many Lands (CMML), et al – these are boots on the ground troopers WHO harmonize and chant the credo – we are our brother's keeper. These are the people who help **keep hope alive!** The hope that, although we may not all get along perfectly but, we as a multiracial, multicultural people who share common space can also share and embrace the uncommon credo: we can all get along!

Speaking of getting along, we have to be moving right along because we have so many other interesting questions to kick around. In the area of challenge-type questions, there is such a variety to tickle our interest that it's almost like an all-you-can-eat buffet or as our Swedish friends call it – Smorgasbord. Let's cool our heels a bit then we can pick and choose a few challenge-type questions from a variety of appetizers and entrees. Are you a buffet or smorgasbord gourmet? You are? Let's go for it!

CHAPTER 12

A SMORGASBORD OF QUESTIONS

Variety of Challenge-type Questions

How is your appetite, are you a weight watcher or calorie counter? No you say you just enjoy delicious eating of a variety of food that looks good, smells good and tastes good? If you asked me that same question I'd give you the same answer. I think the Scandinavians had this in mind when they invented the Smorgasbord or what we in the Continental West re-labeled – Buffet, AKA – all you can eat!

For most of us fans of the all-American Buffet, what tickles our pallet is not the All-that-we-can-eat attraction, but the wide variety of choices among the "endless" delectables at our fingertips. The best I can do at these Buffet spreads is to sample, a bit of this, a bit of that, while keeping an eye on my plate to see if there is sufficient space for another helping of some strange looking appetizer.

Are you saying what does sampling appetizers, entrees, etc. at the Buffet table have to do with challenge driven questions? Well think for a minute, the vast array of challenges is like the wide variety of delectables on the Smorgasbord (Buffet) spread. Our sampling from the spread limits how much we are able to ingest and digest. Do you get that connection? Can't sample everything on the "buffet" table of questions. Some dishes we can only look at and pass by are:

- Why would any person want to sail around the world solo in a sailboat **without a motor for propulsion**?
- Why would a teenager even be allowed to make that dangerous voyage facing the hazards of angry oceans and treacherous seas **all alone**?
- Why would any person want to climb a rock mountain 3,000 feet high with bare hands and feet with **no safety net** to catch his fall?
- Why would any pilot want to test-fly a plane around the world fueled only by solar energy (from the sun) with **no back-up fuel**?
- Why does a man want **to be transgendered** and become able to bear a child – at least want to try?
- Why is there serious research going on to find a way to control time like a stop watch – **stop time and start time**, as we do a stop watch? Why?

On the subject of questions there is such a wide variety of challenges and they all generate matching variety of questions. If you agree, the best we can do is kick around a limited sampling starting with some appetizer-type questions that are triggered by challenges.

If you think about it you will find that <u>challenge</u> is woven into <u>every area of our lives</u>. Some of these challenges are disguised and some are not. Some are personal and require our personal fortitude – strength and spiritual will to overcome. Other types of challenges are not personal – but pack the threat to affect our survival. These are the challenges that others face who sense the compelling need to raise the questions why not, and <u>why not me?</u>

Consider the personal-type challenges we discussed earlier. Sure makes us think that challenge questions are a very important part of our lives. Heard about the story of Malala? Malala's story is so important to our history, our literature and our genre that it deserves a few extra paragraphs in our conversation. Looks like your interest is piqued and you are ready to hear the Malala saga – her story personifies courage, challenge, and the questions that divide these unusual human attributes. Stay tuned – here is the briefing!

CHAPTER 13

WHO IS MALALA?

History's Youngest Nobel Prize Winner

Malala is a Pakistani teenager who is the youngest recipient of a Nobel Peace Prize. Malala joins the pantheon of international notables such as: Dr. Martin Luther King Jr.; Mother Theresa; Dr. Albert Schweitzer and others who spent and gave their lives because they faced down the challenges that threatened personal freedom and personal survival. What does Malala have in common with this iconic group of history makers? It is certainly the question she asked as a little girl of 15 years of age. "<u>Who gives these Taliban fanatics the right to deny us Pakistani girls the freedom to learn and be educated</u>?"

In her rapidly developing and courageous mind she must have thought of the one, two, three reactive questions we all face when challenged: Fright (1); Flight (2); or Fight (3).

Malala not only chose number (3) – Fight. She asked the follow-up question. <u>Why not me?</u> Malala has shown what Taliban terrorists fear most: <u>A little girl with a book,</u> a <u>passion for learning</u>, and some <u>courageous and determined questions</u>. Remember that 19-year-old 15th century heroine of France - Joan of Arc? This was an unusually courageous daughter of France who passed the baton of extreme courage to a Pakistani heroine name Malala.

Two years ago, (2012) in Swat Valley, Pakistan a gunman climbed aboard a pickup truck carrying children home from school and shouted! "Who is Malala?" None of her class-mates pointed her out to this savage "demon." They looked at each other and looked at her. Consider this – the gunman could have hopped off that truck in search of his victim. Can you believe this? Malala stood firmly in the school pick-up truck and replied in <u>three words</u> that are now on their way to become an engravement in Pakistani history and in the memory of all who heard or read about this near tragedy. The three words were: <u>I AM MALALA</u>!

By the grace and mercy of God, I believe Malala was spared because of receiving urgent and skillful care that her near-fatal situation required. Although she will be under medical and surgical care in England for some time to come, she took time out from school to travel to Oslo, Norway where she shared the Peace Prize with a noted Indian children's rights activist – Kailash Satyarthi.

With a spirit of unthinkable courage, this brave teenager answered the question who is Malala? Clearly saying each word in that memorable three-word sentence – "I AM MALALA!" – she did not know, nor could she know some of the events that would follow. Some of them were visits with President Obama (also a Nobel Laureate); The Queen of England; the United Nations General Assembly; and recently on stage in Oslo with world famous admirers of a young Pakistani girl that history will not forget. They came to applaud the youngest person ever to receive such a coveted trophy – the Nobel Peace Prize!

Malala co-wrote a book. The book is titled: I AM MALALA! She gave that three-word answer of indomitable courage that reflects the flame of the human spirit. When people keep on remembering the question: Who is Malala? – they will keep on remembering this courageous young girl consumed by an ideal that burns deeply within the human soul and spirit – the desire to be free and treated equally. In her remarks at the Oslo, Nobel ceremonies – she said these closing words: "I am pretty certain that I am the youngest recipient of the Nobel Peace Prize who still fights with and for her younger brothers and sisters." It seems that in fighting formidable challenge, its not the size of the fighter that wins the battle but the passion and courage in your heart that sustains you in the fight. Malala's saga is unquestionably one for the history books – I mean not just Pakistani history – world history!

I was deeply moved by this sad story emanating from two sides of the same "human coin." On the one side was this deranged question from a Taliban terrorist who did not recognize the answer. Really, who is Malala? Answer! She is an example of the combined grace, mercy and love of God who spared her life. This terrorist did not see that. Perhaps he could not know that! On the other side of the "human coin", Malala in her "spirit" of courage and confidence did not know what I sincerely believe to be an evidence of God's grace, mercy and love shown to her. By the way, there is a third side to that "human coin" (if you look closely, you will see that third side of every coin).

What is that third side of the coin you ask? Well in my humble way of thinking, God spared Malala's life by his favor of mercy, love and grace. God also spared the terrorist's life by His love mercy and grace. So what's my point about the third side. My point is that both can ask similar questions.

Malala's question: Why are you trying to kill me?

Taliban shooter's question: Why am I trying to kill her Why?

May be the deeper questions on that third side of the coin are: are we not our brother's keeper?

My friend here is why? Why! Here comes the good book to give us the precise answer to those puzzling questions: murder springs from the heart of man (without God) but God's word says:

*"For the grace of God has appeared, bringing salva-
tion for all people, training us to renounce ungodli-
ness and worldly passions, and to live self-controlled,
upright, and godly lives in the present age, waiting for
our blessed hope, the appearing of the glory of our
great God and Savior Jesus Christ." (Titus 2:11-13)*

It says that the grace of God that brings salvation has appeared
to all men – teaching us to live soberly (like brothers that we
are) and fearing God (as we should) and live a life of faith in
God and love toward each other. I cannot recall this episode
without thinking that the Taliban shooter and Malala could
both be reached by the power of the Gospel and become
brother and sister in a fellowship of love and endearment.
Have you thought of that?

By the way, remember Son of Sam from the 1970s?
He was a deranged murderer who terrified New York City,
snuffing out many innocent lives. David Berkowitz is currently serving life without parole. In his own words, he writes
in a leaflet titled Son-of-Hope, a detailed account of how he
was transformed – **born again, by the power of the Gospel**.
A spiritual experience of simple faith in Christ that changed
his life and gave him new Hope.

I read that leaflet titled Son-of-Hope, several times. Why
did I you ask? Well, why not? I clearly remember in 1975,
working out of Exxon's Corporate Headquarters Building
in midtown, New York City and leaving the city some late

nights constantly looking over my shoulder never knowing when Son of Sam may strike at random. As we are speaking, I feel in the grip of unspeakable wonder at the power of God's amazing grace in changing this ruthless murderer – Son of Sam into this new man – Son of Hope.

I don't think in our lifetime our world will be rid of Taliban terrorists or their likes, and certainly we hope and pray that people like Malala will be among us carrying the torch as they take a stand for basic human freedoms. The questions they raise will continue to be asked – why? Why not? Why not me? Somewhere in our extended discussion we both may discover the ultimate answer! You say that's a real challenge? Well, it fits so well into the trend of our interchange on questions driven by challenge.

CHAPTER 14

BOOTS ON THE GROUND?

Their mission – to save lives

L eaving the episode of our Pakistani teenage heroine, Malala, behind us for the convenience of our emotions let's get set to consider a few other challenge-type questions. You say her story is so gripping that even when we want to move on, the driving forces of her questions and her answers freeze us in our tracks? In other words you are saying the memories of that courageous saga will not fade anytime soon. I agree, we may come back to visit if you insist, especially since Malala remains in the cross hairs of the Taliban fanatics. In other words, they are out to get her!

For now, let's think of other intrepid and extraordinary people who in military lingo we refer to as <u>Boots-on-the-Ground</u>. These are the ones who deserve a place in our friendly exchange of thoughts about challenge-type questions. They are not on military mission to wipe out the lives of enemy combatants but instead their passion is to <u>save</u> <u>lives</u> and help the needy and helpless.

I know you are not one of them, but there are many of us who are not aware that we human beings have a long, long history of fighting wars. Wars between brothers, (remember Cain and Abel?), wars among family members, wars among villagers, wars in cities, wars among nations and wars even within ourselves – one part of us fighting against the other part of us.

As far back as we can search from the earliest records of our civilization most of these wars were fought with Boots-on-the-Ground. In many cases – hand-to-hand, spear-to-spear, arrow-to-arrow, even to this day despite our sophisticated technology we see news pictures of middle eastern people, boots-on-the-ground, throwing stones at each other. As they say in some southern United States areas – "aint that something?"

Today's battlefield is a terrifying display of weapons of destruction raining down relentless fury of "shock and awe" from the air and sea and land, all propelled by technology you can barely imagine or believe. I can sense by your body language of discomfort that the savagery of war is unsettling to you. It surely leaves little room for comfort or peace within.

You may remember that we discussed earlier how way back in time, wars were fought between groups and nations. Sometime they did this by sending singular representatives to fight and defend their respective sides. They "duked" it out one-on-one! You seemed surprised! There also were kings who went to battle fighting alongside their troops – boots-on-the-ground.

Can you think of how easily and quickly some of our modern wars would be resolved if our heads of states had to be the "boots-on-the-ground" combatants? Instead, what we have now are Commanders-in-chiefs who order battalions of military assets including the best physically endowed youth – male and female to engage in missions of destruction of their fellowmen. These warriors declare victory in the name of the greatest of human virtues – freedom and liberty!

That aside, let's come back to our example of boots-on-the-ground. I'd like to think of the chain effect of challenge-driven questions. I am thinking of the well-known story of two men pitted against each other in boots-on-the-ground combat. The men are dissimilar in physical size and strength. For the smaller of these two, this seemed and impossible challenge!

In the Bible story (1 Sam 17: 49-51) – it was the shepherd boy David with this question: **Is there not a cause?** Here comes that challenge-prompted question again! The story ends, as you may recall, with the power of that courageous question pitted against a seemingly impossible challenge. Goliath was defeated and David in his boots-on-the-ground and one smooth stone from a shepherd's sling, will be remembered as long as giants challenge little shepherd boys like David.

In real time and in recent periods of real life, even as we speak, you can think of some exceptional people who were never deterred or discouraged by challenges. Instead of impossible challenges – they saw <u>Challenging Causes</u>. They hear an inner voice saying – <u>Is there not a cause</u> to be addressed? Is there not the need for urgent action? <u>Why not me</u>?

Some names just popped up in my head. Some of them go way back, further back than you and I can recall. There was David Livingstone of Scotland, a passionate 18th century missionary who saw the challenge of hopelessness and despair in the lives of languishing souls all over the undeveloped areas of Africa.

You might say of Livingstone (reading his memoirs) that he was a pathfinder! He found paths in the African continent where there was not a bit of any trail of missionary outreach before. With a compass in hand and basic explorers' tool box in tow, this physician and explorer weaved his way through the most hostile and treacherous regions of Africa from Cape Town in the south to regions near the Equator. From regions near the Atlantic Ocean to arid areas near the Indian Ocean, relentlessly he soldiered on.

When David Livingstone returned home to Scotland, it is said that he asked that his heart be buried in Africa where he spent almost thirty of his sixty missionary years (1813-1873) of his life – boots-on-the-ground bringing life and hope to people on a continent he never knew, among people he had never met before but found a cause and challenge to which he responded – <u>why not me</u>? Livingstone's question before he launched his near impossible adventure into the crevices of the African continent was quite different than the question raised by Hamlet – Shakespeare's Prince of Denmark, as he waffled almost in mental torture, remember? Yes, that's right – the question was "to be or not to be? For David Livingstone the picture was different, the challenge was different and so was the cause.

I think what we are sensing in our discussion is **the power of the right questions**! If you just imagine Livingstone's musings. He had a clear vision of what was considered the darkest continent on earth. Millions of people enslaving other people. People in darkness socially and spiritually. People without the basics for marginal survival – this was the challenge that prompted Livingstone's questions: <u>Is there not a cause</u>? Next question: why should these appalling conditions persist among my fellow human beings? Who will step up and face this seemingly impossible mission at the cost of personal survival? <u>Who</u>? You just filled in the blank – that linchpin question (who) pops up again – why not me?

Livingstone's linchpin question lingers with us for a host of reasons. One of them is that there is another side to the humanity displayed by some of our fellow human beings. One of the incomparable achievements of these mission-aries of mercy is that their outreach touches not only the day-by-day living conditions of millions of needy people, but they reach out from their hearts and souls with the Bible message of the Gospel.

You will be stunned to hear about people in villages and cities where cannibalism was rampant until the wonderful message of the Gospel shone as a bright light in what seemed to be total darkness in terms human civility, kindness, love and caring for each other. This message has spread and people began to see and feel the almost miraculous changes in their hearts and lives that resulted from this new message. I heard or read somewhere that when David Livingstone returned to his native Scotland, he was physically emaciated and without the use of one arm. You and I can certainly conclude that African lions have no sense of distinction between prey in the wild and an exceptional human being. You can just imagine how those people adore this wonderful, loving, caring, spiritual motivated human being who crossed their path, or better yet – blazed a trail and excavated a path to find them in darkness, distress, dismay, delusioned, and brought them a message of hope, God's love and grace. A Bible message that changed their lives and living.

May I share with you an extended insight into David Livingstone's sacrificial missionary venture into the African continent? Are you wondering why I seem so pensive at the moment – I am thinking this: we humans (both of us included) may not realize the power of the never ending question we keep asking ourselves and others? If you think about it, that the power driving our questions pushes us in many directions. For David Livingstone and others like him it was toward a spiritual direction – the saving of lost souls – then there was the humanitarian passion to help sick people get well even when he got sick from their sometimes-incurable diseases.

May I ask your indulgence as we pause to salute and thank God for the incredible courage, compassion, caring and passionate commitment to spreading the message that packs the power to change the lives of people everywhere. Thank you Dr. David Livingstone and all those you have so impressively inspired. They found traces of your boots-on-the-ground and are blazing new trails even now! They, even now as we take this break to salute these intrepid soldiers of mercy, these boots-on-the-ground battalions, are advancing despite the resistance of the "gates of hell." Their troops are advancing all over violence-riddled areas of our planet. These troops are marching on and will never call retreat.

You ask why this passion, why this sacrificial commitment to help others? Only one answer comes to mind. I think they are still hearing and listening to the words of their Supreme Commander spoken to eleven men from Galilee in Israel. Go you into all the world and spread this <u>word of life</u>. Spread this <u>message of hope</u>. It will rescue the perishing and care for the dying. When Dr. Livingstone was asked what kept him alive during those near-death experiences on the African continent – his reply – "the invisible but guaranteed presence of God every where I was and every place I was." I can see you are quite moved by this compelling power of the question why not? When faced with daunting challenges, and the follow up <u>why not me?</u> when faced with seemingly impossible situations. I am deeply moved as we speak. So here we go, speaking of being moved – let's move on!

CHAPTER 15

SPECTATORS OR DIFFERENCE MAKERS?

If you see something – do you do something?

Not too many decades ago if you were a resident in New York City, living with millions of people shuttling in and out this mega metropolis in a network of transportation systems, you may you remember a culture whose credo was, "<u>Mind your own business, don't get involved!</u>" The thing about this credo was it gave you a false feeling of security. How so you ask? Well, the fact is that while you may feel safe in that moment when you are just "minding your own business" instead of lending a hand or calling for help on behalf of a fellow traveller, surprisingly you may get attacked. Thankfully, you may get rescued because someone came to your aid. A Good Samaritan came by and made the difference between your being left half dead or half alive.

Fortunately, over the years, there has been a great cultural shift in our civil behavior in New York City as well as other world cities.

You see, my friend we did not leave so far behind your conversation about the Paradox of Man, his shifting behavior, sometimes good, sometimes astonishingly good, sometimes the converse – very bad, and sometimes neither – like: don't get involved – just be a spectator!

We remain forever grateful to those whose credo is – <u>we are our brother's keeper</u>, we can make a difference! Who are these you ask? They are more in number than I know about and more than I can recall by names. I just coined a name for these, agents of mercy who we are speaking about. These I call: <u>Difference Makers</u>. These trailblazers all speak the same lingo. They don't say – <u>if you see something say something</u>. The say if you see something <u>do something.</u> They are Difference Makers!

You say what about the spectator types you mentioned earlier. They don't get involved; they only give a casual or furtive glance at what is happening. Ok, I'll oblige and share some brief thoughts about those types of spectators. I am not able to keep the words of the noted English statesman Edmund Burke out of my thoughts. Burke said (paraphrased) the worst of human tragedies occur when good men do nothing! In other words – you see bad things happen and you say nothing and you do nothing.

That's right! You took the words right out of my mouth. World War II and Adolf Hitler you say? No matter where we are on the age scale, the History lessons of World War II should be a necessary part of our education. We have so much to learn from the history of that war. We learn from history that there were many passive spectators who heard the heart wrenching cries for help from people all over the German human landscape. Help and rescue cries came from nearly six million people in utmost distress. Their crime? They were descendants of Abraham. This was an atrocity unparalleled in human history!

Adolf Hitler, the demonic mastermind of the Jewish extermination was enabled big time by "spectators" who offered little or no opposition to this tyrant's mad rage! While the German stampede came from the air, and land, and the sea forged ahead, Europe ran the cover. They found temporary protection from the savage onslaught of the Third Reich – the infamous organization for the destruction of Jews in Germany.

Thankfully, there was another side to this "coin" of human tragedy. What was that side of the coin you are asking? If you think back, or if you flip the pages of history, you will find that in England, one of the surprises of the war was a voice that emerged! No, it was not the voice of an English spectator, it was the voice of an Englishman who remembered the words of one of their national anthems –"Rule, Britannia!

Britannia, rule the waves! Britons shall never, never shall be slaves!"

What a moment of historic fortune for Great Britain that Winston Spencer Churchill emerged from the political confusion of his generation and dazzled the whole world with his announcement. What was that you say? First, I think, from reading his memoirs, he resolved that one man with God's help and human courage, could defeat the mightiest of the German military forces. He felt that <u>one man could make a difference</u> if the nation shared his resolve and passion!

Winston Churchill, who succeeded the waffling, compromising and incompetent Neville Chamberlin, as Prime Minister during the war years, resolved that he would be, could be, and became a <u>Difference Maker.</u> He will never be forgotten in world history. As the people of England ran for cover, they ran and scrambled into underground shelters for personal survival. The German Air Force – Luftwaffe – bombed their cities, towns and villages night and day, 24/7.

Then came – the "Bulldog" of Britain with an unmistakable English Growl. He aroused all England (and the world) as he exclaimed that difference – making the statement that still hangs around in British thoughts even in our post-modern world – yes even today! What was that difference – making statement by the "bulldog" of Britain you ask? He said, (paraphrased) "We will never surrender, no never! We will fight them on land, sea and in the air! We will fight them in the hills and in the valleys, in the streets and on the highways! We will never surrender – No Never! Never! Never!"

That my friend is history's video that shows us the picture of one man who made a difference for his nation and the world as we know it today.

Have you noticed what happened when a nation of spectators watched as nearly six million defenseless people were "executed" because one demonized man – Adolf Hitler, was allowed to run amuck and unrestrained? Then take a look at what happened when one man – a Difference Maker – WINSTON SPENCER CHURCHILL – FOUND HIS VOICE AND FOUND HIS STRIDE IN THE STREETS of London to chant: "BRITS NEVER, NEVER, SHALL BE SLAVES! BRITAIN WILL NEVER SURRENDER TO THE TYRANNY OF GUNS AND BOMBS. BRITS WILL NEVER SURRENDER – NEVER! NEVER! NEVER!"

All of us, in our generation and those preceding us owe to Sir Winston Churchill and those of his grit and valor, expressions of thanks and a salute of unspeakable gratitude for the lessons learned. What are those lessons you ask again? Certainly one lesson is that, one person asking the right question – why not me? – at the right time, can lead a nation to face down and overcome the most impossible challenge despite predictable doom! Thank you Sir Winston!

Well, it seems clear that among the many other lessons would be: our own survival, as human beings, really depends upon those among us who resolve to be <u>Difference Makers</u> and certainly not those who are <u>Spectators</u>.

I have one other thought on this riveting topic of our conversation. Don't second-guess me now, just hear me patiently. Here is my take! The Bible gives us verbal pictures of the whole human race. It covers all nations in all places. It describes all of the human beings as a population of lost souls – Rom. 3:23

"For all have sinned and fall short of the glory of God,"

But it reports wonderful news. The Bible describes this good news as the Gospel. The message from God to us simply stated that the God who created our "First" parents loves us beyond description. To that extent, he did not just watch us human beings make a mess of our civilization, by fighting wars, killing one another in hostile encounters. With the exception of a precious few, we do not present a picture of love and harmony among ourselves. Do you agree? Yes you do, you say?

Here is how the Gospel I referred to changes this sad picture of the behavior of our fellowmen. The words are found in the New Testament Gospel of John 3:16. It says it all! It says:

"For God so loved the world that he gave his one and only Son, that whoever believes in him shall not perish but have eternal life."

104

This well known verse of Scripture put the Lord Jesus in the center of the human universe, where <u>He alone makes the difference</u> between who we are now, and who we can become, not for now only, but forever! Is that about faith and God's grace you ask? That's right, you hit the "bulls eye." Sounds to me like the more we talk the more we are connecting to the Bible! My friend, give that some thought while we come up for a break in the stroll through our scenic QUESTION WONDERLAND!

CHAPTER 16

WHO ARE THE GREATEST GENERATIONS?

The jury is still out

The history of our human experience is not defined by one person – male or female, like: Adam, the first man or Eve, the first woman, or Abraham, the first Jew, or Moses, the first consummate leader, or Alexander the Great or other stellar leaders of this present time.

Historians report events by the achievements of successive generations. They seem to package their records with a perspective that includes emphasis on events unfolding in generations over periods – thirty years approximately – the typical time line of a generation. The historical reports leave us ample room for personal opinions and conclusions. Does that mean we have some room to exchange our opinions on this "conversational" topic in our leisurely stroll through this

Scenic Question Wonderland? Again you are urging me to kick off my opinion on the topic of the Greatest Generation, ok, I'll oblige!

Does the name Tom Brokaw ring a bell? I see you nod your head. Almost everyone in the last three generations has seen or heard Tom's spellbinding coverage of all kinds of local, national and global events, may times reported as breaking news. Tom was a model of responsible and skillful journalism. For many years NBC was Tom Brokaw and Tom Brokaw was NBC. He also had the grace and gravitas to match his reporting talent.

A few years ago, before his retirement from NBC, the City College of New York (CCNY) alumni invited him to deliver the annual lecturer series speech in the Great Campus Hall. I was part of the host group that engaged Mr. Brokaw in conversation before delivery of his speech on the "Greatest Generation." He left us all very impressed especially with his sincerity and humility.

Tom Brokaw left us an impressive legacy of his brilliant thinking. The souvenir he left us before retiring from NBC was a book titled – The Greatest Generation! In his book Mr. Brokaw introduces and makes frequent complimentary references to the generation spawned during the period of the great depression. The main point of the book is that from the generation of the great depression came heroes and heroines that fought bravely, courageously and patriotically gave their last full measure of devotion to preserve our democracy and ensure our free society.

No one will argue with that. I certainly won't. So you say what is my question? Well, by way of our insightful conversation I'd ask this question: what are the criteria for comparing and concluding which or who is the greatest generation? Without disputing any claims about the kudos deserved by Mr. Brokaw's Greatest Generation, I'd like to take a "crab" approach. What's that you ask? Think of how the crab walks – seems he is always doing a sideways or backward walk.

Our present generation and the one preceding spans about fifty to sixty years. During this time we have engaged our military in wars in distant lands to fight for the preservation of freedom for others and indirectly for ourselves. How we assess our victory or defeat is the assignment for the people who write our history. Did you think of other kinds of wars fought and are being fought by the last two or even three generations. What are those you say? Just to name a few: there is the war on poverty and hunger; the war on epidemic infections and communicable diseases, the war on moral and spiritual darkness – the list goes right on.

In our discussion of the question of the greatest generation - I don't apologize for private bias. What's that you ask? It's simply that I rate the accomplishments of these warriors of recent generations a few notches higher than Mr. Brokaw's World War II warriors despite their valor and victories not withstanding the sincere respect and vast debt that we all owe to them. Fact of the matter is – these unsung non-military heroes seldom come to light via popular media. A random sample of organizations that emerged from generations other than the "great generation" comes to mind like: World Vision; Salvation Army; Red Cross; Samaritan Purse; Operation Mobilization; Mercy Ships; Peace Corps; Habitat for Humanity; Food for the Poor; Doctors without Borders; Missionary Aviation Fellowship; America's Keswick for Recovery from Addiction – the list goes much further on and on!

How could I have omitted the huge impact the philanthropies like the Bill & Melinda Gates Foundation that teamed up with Warren Buffet (the two wealthiest men in the world) to provide funding for projects spearheaded and maintained to bring relief and save lives that literally rescue the perishing and care for the dying. Mr. Gates and his wife Melinda of the "Boomer Generation", in my humble opinion and belief, are clear examples of how the God of the Bible controls people. He controls and coordinates the thoughts, actions, emotions and initiatives of people of His choice without their awareness that God is behind all their philanthropic activity. All you need to do is read the Bill and Melinda Gates Story and you will see that the heart of this wonderful woman has been touched by God. Her husband Bill received a contagious touch and responded – Big Time! Read up on their incredible compassion and kindness. They even successfully recruited Warren Buffet to come on board. They also challenged worldwide billionaires to donate significant amounts of their wealth to help the helpless, the hopeless, the sick, and to bring a gleam of light to the darkness of human suffering.

Is it ironic or what – that this is the same Bill Gates, of the generation I mentioned earlier, that turned the key to open the door to the digital world, changing the way we think, live and work. Could it be that some of these seventeen plus billion dollars in the Foundation that funds those humanitarian projects came from his God-inspired genius launching his digital operating systems for global networks. This discussion is really taken off in some unexpected directions. Let me come back to "square one".

So who is the greatest generation, in any nation, (not just the USA) but wherever human beings share space on this constantly rotating carousel we call planet earth? I believe it is the generation(s) that produces people like the Good Samaritan that Jesus described when He asked the question WHO IS THY NEIGHBOR? In the Bible story, this Samaritan travelling a dangerous road from one city to another saw a man by the side of the road described as half dead after an ugly mugging experience. The Samaritan recognized that this languishing victim was avoided or bypassed by others because of the danger of a similar encounter with professional muggers.

Listen to this – this Samaritan, set aside his fears, of being mugged himself, and followed the prompting of his compassionate heart. He realized that although this victim as far as he could tell, was not a person who lived next door, because he was a Samaritan and could not live next to a Jewish man, - this man was a part of his human family – he was his neighbor! The story Jesus told, in the parable, says that the rescue mission ended up by taking the half-dead man to a motel and assuring that his neighbor (perhaps not even knowing his name) would be cared for at his expense. This is a paraphrase of this timeless magnificent parable by Jesus our Lord. What better story to qualify a generation as the greatest. You can check out this iconic story by reading Luke's Gospel Chapter 10: 29-37.

Certainly, you would agree that a generation from which would emerge people like our Good Samaritan – the man who saw another human being in distress and at the point near death, and move forward, despite the challenge of the moment – stepped back and asked why would someone pass him by, why would someone not help him, why not me? That my friend, that is the measure of a person who belongs to the greatest generation.

How can we move on to another challenge driven question without mention of a much bigger picture of that Good Samaritan? I think that I was once like that man on a lonely road of confusion, and despair and I got mugged by the invisible forces of anxiety and fear. This was a time of almost unconscious dilemma and spiritual darkness in my soul. Then a gleam of light shone in, it was the light of the Gospel. A message from the Bible to me – it was for me. It was like the first-aid administered by the Good Samaritan. I felt as if I had been transported – I cannot fully explain. I do know that the Bible verses I was shown in Rom. 10:9 and Rom. 10:13 gripped me securely. I did not understand the theology of those words – I just was ready to accept Jesus as my Savior. The rest of the story may seep out here and there, but this was a powerful experience that changed my life completely and allowed me to be enjoying this amicable conversation with you, my friend.

So again, for me the Greatest Generation must earn their stripes by producing Good Samaritan types – especially like the one who came by to rescue me. Now where do we go from here? We need a break to digest all this you say? OK. Let's sit for a while, and then we can catch our stride and move on.

CHAPTER 17

QUESTIONS
WITH NO ANSWERS?

A question up for grabs

J ust to lighten up our conversation before we resume some more insightful thoughts about a variety of questions. When you are home or other convenient place, do you like to sit and just let your thoughts roam? I love quiet moments. Do you? Meditation moments, I call them. For me they are really my most creative. As I reflect on the difficult puzzles that crossed my path at different stages of my life, every single solution came to me in moments – I call moments of meditation and inspiration. I will concede the limits to my quiet contemplations especially in areas of God's exclusive "secrets." I accept that I'll never find all the answers to some of my puzzling questions. For example, you may be thinking that I am puzzled about some cosmological mysteries of questions regarding man's current pursuit and preparation for a one way trip to Mars although he knows for sure, it will be <u>ONE WAY</u> if he gets there after approximately 150 million miles and about six months of unprecedented space travel. No you say, what could be such a challenge to your thoughts that you are so intensely puzzled and cannot seem to find a comfortable situation.

Well there are quite a few challenge-type questions or puzzles but let me give you just two and then there is a third one that will really eclipse the first two.

In the study of mathematics there are a bundle of seeming brain busters. They will not spoil our friendly conversation. I promise you I will keep it simple. Did you know, or have you thought that the most difficult mathematical concepts – the tools of all science – are really <u>patterns in nature</u>? Did I say patterns in nature or patterns of nature? No, my friend I said (in) not (of) nature to be really precise and in line with what I believe. What's that you ask? Very simply: here it is! All (in) nature is conceived, designed and maintained by God. All the Science –Technology – the work in progress as we speak come from God's creative genius. So what are my first two of three selected puzzles that keeps me mentally grappling?

The first one, oh so simple, but wait till I ask you to take a crack at it. You may say I am no mathematician. Well, my friend, I am no Isaac Newton, John Von Neumann, or Blaise Pascal either. So it's surprisingly simple – so it seems – but the puzzle is deceptively elusive.

I know you can't wait to hear the puzzle. You must be real good at mathematics. Here it is: remember Pi (p)? That's the Greek letter that in mathematics (Elementary/High School) stands for the ratio of the circumference of a circle to its diameter. Remember the approximation of that ratio - 22/7 or 3.14285714285714---. That is the puzzle! The remainder in the ratio behaves mysteriously increasing up and down in quantity with no predictable sequence. Unlike a recurring decimal which you can predict to keep on going with the same repeated value, or the Fibonacci numbers that repeat themselves in predictable patterns as they progress. Not so with p. Pie eludes all mankind! Since our forbears discovered the Geometry of the circle and applied it to make their first wheel, this ratio has baffled the best brains. Well what's the mystery of p? No human being, or any artificial intelligence (AI) to date has solved nature's riddle of p.

Looks like you like a real challenge. Here is a good one for you to tackle – why not? Why not you? – You should ask! Did I not say there was another puzzling question in the realm of nature that is a real mental "woodpecker" and a stubborn challenge? What's that you ask? Again it seems simple. Here it is. The problem of <u>zero</u> and <u>one</u>. Briefly, and really – this number zero is a cornerstone in mathematics. Let's keep it simple. Seriously, if zero is unethically or carelessly used it can result in extreme poverty or excessive wealth. You smile? Try this next time you write a check - in the box that you enter the dollar amount write 1,000,000 to be paid against the balance in your account which has (hopefully) in excess of 1,000,000. Those zeroes mean a lot. They are a measure of your financial treasure. If you mistakenly remove the number one in front of the zero – there you go – those zeros mean nothing. You have gone from "riches to rags." Now let's say your flip to the next check on the pad and write in the amount box: 000,000,1 what did those same zeroes do? Not much to your financial treasury, but to the receiver – they received the mysterious effect of zero although you wrote the number one in a different place. Wow! You say, better watch how I write those zeros on my checks.

Now, are you ready for this? Let's see another mystery of zero. Let's say – you take the simple Arithmetic example of raising numbers to powers as in the case of the number 2 raised to the power of 1: gives us (2X1) = 2; then the number 2 raised to the power of 2 gives us (2X2) = 4, and 2 raised to the power of 3 (2X2X2) = 8. But look what happens when you apply the <u>mysterious zero</u> to what you just did. In each case if you replace the "power raised" by zero. What do you think you get (when you remember that any number X 0 = 0). What do you get? Well you say the answer has to be zero. Sorry, my dear friend you must know by now that I would say nothing to embarrass either of us. The answer to the question regarding that example of zero is not zero as it appears. No you say? No, that's why this simple mathematical mystery remains a puzzle eluding all our ancestors and both of us as well. The answer is not zero; the <u>answer is the number 1.</u> The number 1! You can check it out on any calculator performing this mathematical operation. Does it surprise you that smart computer, smart phones and all the smartest digital devices operate on a platform of the binary number system of - zero and 1. So the unsolved mathematical mystery of all time really says that proof or not, believe it or not: any number from zero to infinity raised to the zero power is ONE UNIT! As we keep talking we may get further insight into the mystery. What was the third puzzle you have been grappling with that you mentioned earlier you ask?

You will really be surprised that this third puzzle exceeds those two we just discussed. It puts those math puzzles we have been discussing in the back seat of all the challenging questions crossing the mind of man.

Have you thought that the greatest puzzle of man is – Man! Yes Man himself! I have struggled so much with this mystery of Man that in my previous book titled: "What Are You Thinking?" I devoted an entire chapter to the topic of the "Duality of Man."

You say you can't wait to hear that discussion on the puzzle of man? I'd like to hear your thoughts on this fascinating topic. So let's take a minute to look around a bit at these alluring sceneries around here in the serenity of this Question Wonderland. We can now kick around some questions on this mystery of man. Remember the puzzle – the duality of his nature. Remember, we will be including ourselves as part of the family of man.

PART 3

QUESTIONS DRIVEN
BY CREATIVE INSIGHTS

CHAPTER 18

IS MAN A PARADOX?

Who is this man?

You would think from our recent conversation on the "mystery" in the behavior of numbers like <u>zero</u> (0) and <u>one</u> (1) and also the irrational result of the ratio of the circumference of a circle to its diameter - Pie P, that we would put this challenge of unsolved mystery behind us. What challenge you ask? Did you come up with some answers to those number mysteries during the rest break? No, you did not, you say?

Here is my question to you – why are we going from one set of puzzling questions to another, when we did not seem to have a clue in finding answers to those elusive ticklers? The fact that you wish to talk a bit about the Paradox of Man – the contradictions in his nature – the mystery of his actions, answers my question about why we want to extend a discussion on the nature of this topic has been a puzzle of the ages.

What is the answer to this puzzle? Somehow, I think it is in the nature of man not to be overcome by challenge, but to overcome challenges no matter how large in scope and impossible in appearance. That's why we are pecking away at the age-old question about the Paradox of Man. His mysterious nature sometimes described as a conundrum.

John Donne, an English 18th century writer and poet gave us a sketch of man a being a part of a large family sharing space on a continent, each depending on and supporting each other. He presented then the thought that no man (or woman) is an island separated by calm seas, under blue skies all unto ourselves in a singular life style. His poetic thought was that we are a family of human beings sharing common space and we should act like that. How is that? We should look out for each other, love each other, care for each other – we came from the Great Creator and a common ancestry! You smile and expect me to go back to the Bible for support of my statement. Well you are half right. I will make that reference later but for now I'd like to share a few examples about the Paradox of man before we move on.

For example, remember our discussion about David Livingstone and his thirty years of unbelievable missionary saga among the African people. It makes you cringe when you read of the repeated skirmishes that he had with certain and sudden death in his efforts to minister to body and soul. But Livingstone never called retreat in his one-man battle to save lives. He used his medical skills and evangelistic message to bring spiritual life and light in a "dark" continent by sharing the Gospel of the Grace of God and salvation through faith in our Lord Jesus Christ.

I am deeply moved just thinking of how one man who heard a call, (as we all should hear) to rescue the perishing and care for the dying literally put his life on the line to rescue others in distress and despair. He just kept asking, why not me?

Do you realize that at the same time that David Livingstone was blazing those dangerous trails, and was mauled by wild beasts in the African jungle, there was another movement supporting the status quo of colonization and its companion of colonial slavery? The movement was going full blast among his own fellow citizens back in the United Kingdom.

So, although there were human beings of that period who wanted to enslave others of the FAMILY OF MAN as long as they could and for obvious reasons, there were men like William Wilberforce and others who found their stride and raised their voices against the tyranny of man against his fellowman.

By the way, did you know that a voice that was heard and heeded with great respect, on the issue of slave abolition was that of a battle-worn and tireless Scotsman – David Livingstone? Can you imagine – that from the same community of men who vowed to continue slavery – one man went forth to rescue the perishing and help to free the slaves – by the life changing message of the Gospel? From that same community of his fellowmen there are those who were willing to stifle their human compassion and make all kinds of defenseless arguments to support the commercial benefits from the slave industry. What a shame! What a shame!

Here is another timely example of the Paradox of Man. Think of the recently emerged group of mid-eastern terrorists calling themselves ISIS and Boko Haram. I can see, from your squirming body language, that their atrocities give you the chills. I share those emotions. I understand!

Here is my take on these terrorists groups and others like them. I think of them as from a common human ancestry, they are our brothers and sisters. As human beings we descended from the same original parents. Yes, my friend at different times in our long and troubled history some have gone viral in their so-called holy war in defense of Religion. We all grieve as we think of the reported innocent victims left in the wake of these merciless marauders.

Do you know that despite these grotesque beheadings and live incineration of their victims, there are among these terrorists some who have come to faith in Christ by contact with the message of the Gospel? These converts as we speak, are seeking to show the terrorists that God did not create us to fight and kill each other but awake to each day with a listening ear to His message of life and hope directed at every single one of us.

What is that message you are asking? The message is simply this: <u>WE ARE OUR BROTHER'S KEEPER</u>! <u>Not our brother's killers.</u> It's a message of peace - not war! It may surprise you to discover that (though not widely published) there are converted Muslims spreading the life-changing message of the glorious Gospel of the Grace of God that brings salvation to all mankind. Incidentally, my friend whereas we talked earlier about the human brotherhood of man and the Paradox or contradictions in his nature, there is good news! I am thinking of the refreshing good news that the Bible presents. What's that? You seem interested. Well, just take a look here it says in the New Testament in Rom. 10:13 – here, it says: Anyone who calls on the Name of the Lord Jesus shall be saved. This my dear friend, is the key insight into the mystery of the Paradox of Man. He can be an instrument of death and destruction or he can be an agent of life and liberation. It should give us some relief as we think of those who represent the good side of the Paradox of Man.

How can we fix the bad side of the same man? My answer may surprise you. What's that you ask? Here is my answer: the way I got fixed! I came in simple faith to the Word of God – The Bible – then I followed the instructions found in Rom 10:13

"For, Everyone who calls on the name of the Lord will be saved."

That's it? That's exactly it! You want to hear more about that. No problem. This topic will surely pop up as we carry on our questions about the strangeness in the nature of man. What a question – WHO IS THIS MAN?

CHAPTER 19

WHO AM I?

Ever asked this question?

E arlier in our conversation we mentioned that questions were embedded in our human "system" – in the spirit of man, and are unique to our species – remember? We also said and agreed that these questions, in astounding variety, flow through our thoughts like an unending stream that gurgles along as it wends it way in a path that seems to have no end.

We have just finished asking one of the most astute questions that the human mind can handle: who is man? The answers we accepted (I did) were necessary and sufficient. What say you? You were impressed that the Bible had so many answers to so many different questions, you say? That's a very unusual experience we are having. We are able to find comfort and bonding levels in our conversation. We have no difficulty in showing sincere respect for each other's views.

With that in mind, I think we are ready to press a very sensitive and personal button with the question: Who am I?

I think, most of us as we move along in life, take some clips of time to do what we now call "mindfulness." This is the new buzzword for: meditation, or sometimes we may prefer to call it reminiscence. Just thinking back a bit. You like that you say?

Let me share with you one of the things I remember most from my childhood days. I remember being introduced by my parents to adults and without missing a beat they would trot out the questions that had become so predictable that I memorized the answers. On one occasion, I think I gave the answer, before the lady asked me her questions.

I know that you are itching to hear the predictable questions these strangers would ask me. Well, here they are! The questions usually start with, what is your name, and age then, sometimes where do you go to school, then how are you doing in school, then here is the one that they always left for the last, but they never failed to ask! What do you want to do when you grow up?

Even at that "tender" age most kids know how to tell people what they want to hear. By the way, what I really wanted to say to them is: I don't even know you, so why do you want me to answer those very personal and private questions. But kids are smarter than most people think. So you tell them what they want to hear. So what did you tell them you are asking? As I recall, I'd tell different people different things. I kept growing up and my developing mind kept soaking up new information and observing people doing "fascinating" things. I remember one thing clearly. Never did I put all my eggs in one basket in answering the question of <u>what I wanted to do when I grew up</u>. I always kept three baskets handy. So, I would answer this way: either a Medical Doctor; an Engineer; or an Airline Pilot.

Truth be told at that age I was genuinely fascinated with the accomplishment and success of these people in those professions.

One of the pleasures and treasurers of childhood, despite my poverty with which I was truly blessed, is that you are allowed all the imagination and fantasizing of your busy little mind. Later on in life, as I think of those well meaning people, I wonder if they understood their questions. Did they think that who I became when I grew up would be who <u>I would become as a person</u>, as a functional person with the life-long goal to serve and help others without the motivation for fame or fortune. As I grew older, it took awhile for me to put in proper perspective the difference between who I am, and what I did as a professional person. The better perspective, I thought was to consider that who I am had little or nothing to do with attaining any of those answers that I gave when asked what do you want to do when you grow up.

So what is your thought about the question: who am I? you want me to expand the discussion. Ok I'll oblige! We have agreed to use the Bible as our ultimate reference for all our questions. The Bible gives a complete description of all human siblings, (brothers and sisters) in the human family. It should not surprise you that the Bible in its comprehensive coverage of all time, all things, everywhere uses words that are not popular or embraced in our day-to-day conversations. If we ask the question <u>who am I</u> and listen to the Bible answer, we may be pleasantly or even unpleasantly surprised that, it has nothing to do with – what we do for a living. So what does it say about – who am I?

Let's read a few clips together: in Rom. 5:12, right here we read (paraphrased) these words together:

"Therefore, just as sin entered the world, through one man, (Adam) and death by sin, so death was passed upon all men, <u>making us all sinners.</u>"

In Rom. 1:22-23 we read, for all <u>are sinners</u> and have not met God's requirements stated in His laws. The Bible, as we have noticed, has simple and direct ways of answering the most complicated questions including – who am I? It also states that in God's expression of love for the sinful descendants of Adam, who we are, He sent His Son Jesus Christ down to planet earth to deliver the glorious message of the of the Gospel. He also came to earth to make eternal salvation available for all mankind.

It is that message of power; grace and mercy that changed my whole life and made me become <u>who I am</u>.

Its that life-changing experience that made me realize that although I accomplished some of my youthful fantasies (and much more). I could never become the person I am now no matter how hard I tried <u>without a miracle</u>. Have you ever heard this song: "it took a miracle to hang the world in space, it took a miracle to put the stars in place, but when he saved my soul, cleansed and made me whole, it took a miracle of love and grace." So did I answer your question – who am I? <u>I am the product of God's miracle of love and grace</u>. This spiritual miracle changed my whole life and brought me to a point in my life's journey where I was urged to make this stroll with you through this Question Wonderland. As we head toward the exit, in a few miles, I'd be glad to step back to this very important personal question. Do you say, you are doing some introspection right now, asking yourself – who am I? That's right on! For now, let's move right along – some more creative questions.

CHAPTER 20

WHO IS GOD?

Can we know Him?

D o you think a question like "who is God" is too abstract or even necessary for us to discuss? You say no! I think it's a useful and perhaps even necessary because we both may learn something. That is if we stay away from the age-old philosophical opinions of the so-called enlightened thinkers. In other words – keep it simple, so we can really learn something we can apply to our lives.

We can approach this seeming impossible-to-answer question in two ways: we could say – I know who He is, or I don't know who He is. If we say we don't know who God is then we may discover that there is little or <u>no excuse</u> for our ignorance. We may even find out that there are consequences for our "private" ignorance. There is one sure rescue from this dilemma of ignorance regarding who God is. Yes my friend, I can't tell you how impressed I am by your intelligence and mental focus. Why did you think the Bible would help us resolve this dilemma of ignorance about who is God?

You say, because it seems to have all the answers that the mind of man can ever conceive? My friend you are right on the money with that comment! To the point of the expression – "I don't know who God is", we have specific written information all over the Bible in both Old and New Testaments. I know you have heard of or perhaps are familiar with some of the Psalms. "The Lord is my Shepherd" – the 23rd Psalm is known nearly everywhere in every language. You say, that's one of your favorites. Mine also. But here is another favorite of mine that speaks directly to the point of not having any excuse for not knowing who God is. In Psalm 19: 1-3 we read:

> *"The heavens declare the glory of God; the skies proclaim the work of his hands. Day after day they pour forth speech; night after night they reveal knowledge. They have no speech, they use no words; no sound is heard from them."*

These words from the Bible are clear and complete. Now, look at this verse in Isaiah 45:18:

> *"For thus saith the Lord that created the heavens; God Himself that formed the earth and made it; He established it, He created it not in vain, He formed it*

to be inhabited; <u>I AM THE LORD; AND THERE IS</u>
<u>NONE ELSE.</u>*"*

Wow! You say: I say Amen! I think that is a statement from
the Holy Scriptures that wipes away any trace of ignorance
(not knowing) about who God is. I am so pleased with your
affirmation about the reliability of the Bible.

On the other hand, if you already know who God is, then
you can better appreciate the question. You immediately
begin to think of how you were introduced to this Creator
God! What an awesome and amazing thought. The Great
Creator God became our (my) Savior. That's how I came to
know <u>who God is</u>! Through His Word and His Holy Spirit,
I am as we speak, learning more and more about who He
really is. There is never enough time to talk about what the
Bible reveals about God. When you discover who God is,
no matter how much time you have in your whole life, it is
never enough to emote about the wonder, the majesty, the
mystery, the mercy, the grace, the love, the omniscience, the
omnipotence et al of the God of the Holy Scriptures, who
from Genesis to Revelation, (the first and the last books of the
Bible) presents Himself as the incomparable -- I AM!

And you ask, how did I get introduced to Him? Simply
by accepting His offer of love and grace. By following the
simple steps of faith given in Rom. 10:9 and Rom. 10:13
That we discussed earlier.

"If you declare with your mouth, "Jesus is Lord," and believe in your heart that God raised him from the dead, you will be saved. For, "Everyone who calls on the name of the Lord will be saved."

My friend, the only reason we are having this engaging conversation is because many years ago I was introduced to my beloved Savior via the reading of the Scriptures that I just shared. I do not know now, all there is to know about who God is (no one does) but I'll say this from the little I know, since I have trusted and committed my life to Him, the best words I can think of, since my own words are so insufficient, are those of the great Apostle Peter (New Testament) who said that though we do not see Him, yet, by faith, we rejoice with joy inexpressible (1 Peter 1:8). Keep this question, "WHO IS GOD" in mind: I am sure it will pop up again before we exit this beautiful Question Wonderland.

CHAPTER 21

WHERE IS GOD?

Ever heard this question?

This "Question Wonderland" environment is made to order for peaceful and insightful conversation. It also is a glove fit for the creative exchange of various topics. Have you also noticed how the stream of questions and topics have been flowing smoothly from curiosity, to challenge, and it seems we are set up for a segue into the areas of <u>creativity</u> and <u>contemplation</u>. What say you? You say that you were having similar thoughts? Is that what they call mental telepathy or some such thing?

If we think about it, a few minutes ago we have just shared about God – the Creator, calling out his creature – Adam – with his first question: Adam – <u>where are you</u>? I think we learned a lot from the insights we shared in that discussion. It should not surprise you, that in our flow of <u>creativity</u>, that we would include a bit about man asking the question: <u>where is God</u>!

Does it not seem amazing to you that the uniqueness of the human mind is its creativeness – the God-given ability to imagine, conceive, probe, analyze, explore, contemplate, invent and <u>relentlessly ask questions</u>. Nothing is off limits to these offspring of Adam and Eve! Remember Adam learned to ask questions by imitating his Creator.

So here we come, with a bucket full of creative questions. Do you notice that people don't verbalize or say out loud some questions that float around in their thoughts? Yes I agree with you, when you say that they are not sure how they may be perceived if they raise certain issues by way of questions. The trickiest and most sensitive among all the issues are politics and religion. I think religion is so broad in diversity that most people avoid it like the proverbial plague. How many times have you heard anyone ask the question: where is God? It's funny how things pop in and out of your mind. Sometime ago, I heard a story about two boys in a Sunday School class. These kids ask the funniest questions. I think this one is over the top. These two brothers were attentively listening to their teacher following her lesson plan, when the church Pastor stopped by. He surprised both teacher and students with the pop quiz question: Where is God?

The boys looked at the teacher, then looked quickly at the Pastor and said – let's get out of here as fast as we can – they sure did. When their parents caught up with them to ask why did they run out of the Sunday School class – they promptly responded by saying that: "If the church Pastor did not know where God was, why was he asking us." We are only Sunday School kids. They went on to say that they were afraid the Pastor, not knowing where God was, would call on them to find Him. I still chuckle when I recall the story.

We both enjoyed a bit of levity from that tale of the two brothers in Sunday School. If you think of the reaction of the boys – its really funny! There is another side to that anecdote. Many, many of us have a similar view of God. The boys reasoned – How can we tell if God is in America or Europe? If He were in America – in which State and in which city and where in the city or town or village could we locate Him. If we did, could we see Him. Their problem with that question: you, see they needed a better <u>understanding of who God is</u>.

May I share a thought with you that has to do with why I have an unshakable faith in the God of the Bible. From the Bible, I learn that God has numerous <u>attributes</u>. For example: His love, mercy, holiness, and many others. Some of these we share on a human level. Hear this, there are (3) three, that I call the Big 3Os that no human being can attain or claim. They are <u>His Omnipotence, His Omnipresence and His Omniscience</u>.

We talked very briefly about His Omniscience, regarding knowing exactly where Adam was, in the Garden of Eden, despite the question God asked him – Adam – where are you? Do you see where I am going my friend? You do! Thank you.

This was the problem for the Sunday School boys. This attribute of God's Omnipresence is not easily understood but it is clearly declared in the Bible.

Are you excited about the Bible? I am beyond words? The Bible is ahead of the curve on every subject known to man – including this very mysterious concept of God's Omnipresence. Here is a simple example: in the Acts of the Apostles (Acts 1:9) we have the historic record of the ascension of our Lord Jesus. We also have an inspired confirmation of that event and His return to heaven – (Heb. 4:14). In addition we have a record of the words of Jesus (Matt.28: 19-21) before His ascension: clearly stating that His presence would be with these Apostles (missionaries) everywhere they go. So here we have the Bible giving us clear examples of the meaning and reality of God's Omnipresence as a unique and distinct attribute of God.

This, my friend answers the question of ages past and answers the question of the Sunday School brothers who ran away in fright because they were asked the impossible question – Where is God? There is one more point, if I may. If we really believed in the Omnipresence of God, can you imagine the difference it would make in the way we live on this tiny bit of real estate where we share common space? Are you asking if God's Omnipresence applies to us here as we stroll thru Question Wonderland? I defer to you for the answer.

Here is what I am thinking as we move right along. We all have moments of fear for various reasons, but if we put our faith in our Lord and Savior, we can be sure of his Omnipresence, that is just like the invisible air we breathe to sustain life. His invisible presence is guaranteed. We can face the unknown future with confidence in His invisible presence in all places and at all times. Speaking of times, perhaps we should pause a few minutes to digest some of these sobering insights.

CHAPTER 22

DID GOD ASK
THAT QUESTION?

Can we answer that question?

J ust a few moments ago before we took a break to recharge our "Question Batteries", we were speaking so admiringly about those Difference Makers. They all seem to ask the right questions at the right time and then aggressively take action to confront the prevailing challenge. Even if we sometimes forget their exceptional courage, history will keep their memory alive.

Did you ever think that for the rest of us, without exception, there is something automatic within ourselves that drives us like a question machine asking questions non-stop from we awake to the time we go to sleep? It seems that we are having a ball kicking around questions rooted in curiosity and challenge. I have been stimulated by these exchanges.

Have you? They really are eye-openers, and some are even eye-poppers! In the mix of our conversation we want to also include questions that float around in our minds that we don't even share with others.

Do you agree that the rapport we have developed during this Question Wonderland stroll makes it easy for us to talk about even the most sensitive questions? You say that you were thinking the same thing! Have you ever thought how special we are as human beings? Nowhere else in the universe are there "siblings" like ourselves with the unique ability to ask questions. Did you know that? Are you saying, what about the rapidly developing technology in Artificial Intelligence (AI)? I see you are tuned into that cutting edge exploration. Really, I am fascinated by this uniqueness in our species to ASK QUESTIONS! In my book titled "WHAT ARE YOU THINKING?" I devoted a chapter to explaining the limits of (AI). I mentioned that this ability to originate questions was embedded in the architecture of the human spirit by his Creator – the Almighty God!

Have you ever wondered or thought why God asked His very first question to man? You say, why did God have to ask the creature He created any kind of question. Does not God know all the answers? That's an intelligent and excellent point! Would you like my briefing on that point? Well, here are my thoughts.

If you recall from reading the record in the first book of the Bible – Genesis in chapter three, there is a brief dialogue between the Creator – God and His creature Adam. The setting is a pristine environment. It was so exquisite that frequently it is described as paradise. In this environment, God gave clear and <u>CAUTIONARY</u> instructions to Adam. He told him what he could and should do with specific emphasis on the consequence of disobedience.

As you will recall, from this well known narrative, Adam and his wife Eve went into hiding. I think we have to conclude that they did not know then what we know now about one of the key attributes of God. What's that you are asking? My friend, all the attributes of God are awe-inspiring. This one – His OMNISCIENCE is no exception.

Can you imagine that Adam thought he could hide from God, and for how long? Every time I think of the OMNISCIENCE of God, I think of a few paraphrased words of Scripture:

> "*I know the thoughts that come into your mind "every one of them*." (Ez.11:5)

> "*The darkness hideth not from thee - darkness and light are both alike to thee*." (Ps. 139:12)

> "*Before you were formed in the womb I knew you, and before you were born I chose you to be my prophet*." (Jer. 1:5)

These are only a few sample statements of God's Omniscience. If you believe this – you do? I do too! Then it must be real scary if you are doing something disobedient, knowing that you can't hide for long. Back to the question of why was the God of creation who is omniscient, knowing everything, why was he asking Adam – where are you? Let me share my thoughts about the reasons for that question in a few short steps: first, to show Adam that its futile to hide from his Creator – He is omniscient! Next, to show Adam his state of being afraid was a consequence of his disobedience, and finally, that Adam had now crossed the line from state of pure innocence into a landscape of fear!

As I read this passage over and over to see what I might learn, I thought that Adam did not answer God's question. God asked him where he was. He answered, I was afraid because I was naked and I hid myself. He did not say where he was hiding. Do you think he understood the question God asked? As we are speaking I think Adam understood the question and gave the right answer. How is that you are asking?

Think this: Adam knew that by his disobedience that he lost his place in the STATE OF INNOCENCE (PURE AND WITHOUT SIN) and crossed the line into the STATE OF FEAR. Please pay attention to his answer – The question: where are you? His answer: I am afraid – I am in the state of fear: that's where I am! What an appalling shift from innocence to fear. You know the rest of the story! Adam and Eve were expelled from paradise but they never forgot that question neither did God forget them. Adam learned the importance of questions from his Creator and so should we. From that question Adam learned that God – the loving and almighty and compassionate God says what he means: don't eat of the tree of knowledge of good and evil. If you do – you will be sure to die!

He also learned that God means what he says! That's why they were expelled. He also learned why we will never stop asking questions from awake to sleep time. Why you ask? Because in the intricate details of God's meticulous creation of man, He embedded in his "essence" the faculty to ask questions without which we would not have the civilization we enjoy today and we would not be forever asking questions.

Wherever you are in the landscape of your daily life you can hear the echoes of that first question from the Creator God to our ancestor – Adam: "Where are you?" I am sure answers to that personal question will come to mind as we keep talking. So let's keep moving right along!

CHAPTER 23

THE MOST
IMPORTANT QUESTION

Ever asked that personal question?

Well, well, I almost want to suggest that we make a U-turn that would delay our exit from the idyllic Imaginary Question Wonderland. Where did the time go? Perhaps the same place time always goes since it has been coming and going.

Since we started this stroll together it has been like that dream vacation. They say the ideal vacation is the one where you are excited in the preparation for it, you are delighted in the enjoyment of it, and you are joyful in your reflections about it. Whether it's a cruise or some other exotic leisure excursion. The reflections can be so real and delightful especially as we review those digital pictures and other memorabilia. Then there is the bonding with family and friends – old and new friends. What a reward for that well deserved get-away we affectionately call <u>VACATION</u>!

I can see that you get my drift when I mentioned vacation bonding. I have a sense that even before we started this trip in the "Question Wonderland," we were both prepared for these interesting conversations we have been having. This could not happen without the bonding we formed as we listened to each other with mutual respect and willingness to disagree if necessary, without rancor.

I certainly enjoyed the scope and coverage of our inquisitive and stimulating thoughts. Did you? You say that I took the words right out of your mouth? That's what I call real bonding! Like that that ideal vacation we just discussed, we should be ready for some delightful reflections. If you wish we could take turns reflecting on random questions we have been discussing. Again you say that I should go ahead! Again I'll defer to you and will do just that.

If you recall we started our wonderland stroll informally agreed on a simple template to frame our questions. We noticed that most questions we ask on a daily basis breakout in three main areas: <u>Curiosity; Challenge and Creativity</u>. We left Creativity for last because it included many personal-type questions. In the area of <u>Curiosity</u>: we reached back into antiquity to find a Biblical icon named JOB. Remember him? We noticed that many questions were and still are, asked about God's "fairness" to JOB seeing he had lived such a remarkable life. We were focused not on questions about him, but also questions that he asked! We marveled at the astuteness of his questions. The questions he raised made us think that we should look around more closely and ask more incisive questions.

An example of the driving force of curiosity questions is the Mars One project that is in progress as we speak. The probe crawling around at a snail's pace on the craggy terrain of the red planet approximately 150 million miles away from earth, as you may remember, is called <u>Curiosity</u>! You say – couldn't find a better name? I agree! Speaking of mars, we also were so amazed at the – let's say - insanity of some fairly intelligent people who are now scrambling to be among the first humans to attempt a <u>one way trip to mars</u>! Think I remember a book I read some time ago – titled "Men are from Mars." I don't think women would drudge up such a crazy idea. You say some women have signed up for the trip. I don't think they will show up!

Then we really searched our compassionate hearts as we extensively discussed Rodney King's question – "can we all get along?" The bottom line question was not: can we all get along? But are we our brother's keeper? We agreed that the second question should be answered before we can answer Rodney King's question – can we all get along?

Then we discussed Malala, that very, very courageous and valiant Pakistani teenager – the youngest ever to receive a Nobel Peace Prize. History has already reserved a place for her in the archives of valor and her story is not nearly finished! We pray that she survives the Taliban's determination to hunt her down and take her out.

Among the highlights of other questions were those of "Boots-on-the-ground" and also, "The Greatest Generation." You say you have a mental list of some other topical questions we discussed? What are they? Let's see what you jotted down that caught your special interest. Your questions topics you jotted down are:

- Questions without answers
- Paradox of Man?
- Who is this Man?
- Where is God?
- Who am I?
- Spectators or Difference Makers?
- The sky is no limit
- Difference strokes for different folks

Well, we can't do a total recap but I am sure after our exit of the "Wonderland" many of our insightful discussions on these widely scoped questions will be long remembered.

By the way, let's slow down a bit. Can you help me hold back the time? Some place I heard that all good things come to pass or come to an end. I can see the "Wonderland" exit getting closer and closer. We should now be making room in these limited moments of our conversation for a personal question or two. Let's park here a few minutes as we gather our thoughts and share some bonding moments.

CHAPTER 24

WHERE ARE WE HEADED?

Is there certainty about eternity?

There has never been and never will be any device of any kind that squelches the appetite of our fellow mortals in the quest for answers to all kinds of questions.

Our questioning temperament of intrepidness, courage and stubbornness have been deeply engraved in the core of our being. I wonder if you share my quandary about that strange mystique of our global siblings? What's that mystique you ask? Well, here is what baffles me: I am amazed at the genius of my fellowmen. They have for so many succeeding generations, questioned their way into areas of <u>curiosity,</u> <u>challenge</u> and <u>creativity</u> where there seems to be no possible answers. There seems to be no barriers of impossibility that their questions could not penetrate or <u>confront</u>. We salute these heroes of the past and even as we speak they are working through the "hard" questions confronting us today. They are pressing on even though some of these questions are about the unknowable future. Other more elusive questions are about the Mystery of Eternity!

How can anyone be really certain about Eternity? You ask? It's amazing that there are miracles or mysteries of our time that receive so little publicity. I consider a miracle something that you cannot explain and you can hardly believe even when you see it or hear about it. That's my spin on a miracle or mystery. What's yours? There you go again asking me to go ahead of you. I'll keep deferring to you as you wish.

There is one miracle that's always on the tip of my tongue. You remember I shared with you earlier one of my favorite choruses: "It took a miracle to hang the world in space, it took a miracle to put the stars in place, but when He (the Lord Jesus) saved my life, it took a miracle of love and grace." that in a nutshell is my personal miracle.

Let me share with you another miracle. Did you ever hear the story of Stephen Hawking? The story of Stephen Hawking will remain in my thoughts forever as a modern miracle. This youthful, and unusually brilliant, graduate of Cambridge University in England, fell victim to ALS (Amyotrophic Lateral Sclerosis) in the infancy of his cosmologist career. He was by wide acclaim – successor to Albert Einstein in the abstract world of Theoretical Physics.

The impact of his disability, kept him bound to a wheelchair and left him physically crippled. Although most of his normal physical functions are disabled, he has come a long way to reach his 73rd birthday.

I call it a miracle that medical prognosis gave him two years to live after the ALS diagnosis, but he exceeded that time by more that half a century. I call that miraculous. Don't you?

Another dimension of that miracle is the fact that, he has to be assisted in all his physical functions, yet the thinking area of his brain remains an amazement to the world of Science. The Stephen Hawking story is so awe-inspiring that it gives you chills when you realize that his existence and genius are clearly a package of miracles. Here is another part of his miracle package: a cutting edge set of digital devices including a synthesizer, enables his questions, his propositions, and his brilliant search for answers to be transmitted and reduced to legible script.

Have you read Stephen Hawking's book titled – "A Brief History of Time?" You haven't, you say? In his famous work explaining the Physics of Time, and how the Universe works, can you believe what is <u>his most puzzling question</u>? You hit another bull's eye - that's exactly right! His elusive question is about <u>the certainty of eternity</u>! I am not at all surprised that Hollywood picked up the Stephen Hawking story and turned it into a high demand cinema production. "The Theory of Everything," as a documentary of sorts, gives little credit to the "miracle package" I referred to earlier.

My fascination with Dr. Hawking started back in the mid 1970's when the Journal of Science featured his original discovery of "Black Hole" in the universe. As an Engineering student at the City College of New York (back in the early 60s), I was assigned an honors project that required a detailed analysis and explanation of Albert Einstein's famous Theory of Relativity. I was amply rewarded for my effort. I became very mesmerized by the research and literally awe struck in the presentation of my final work. My greatest reward was <u>my mind stretch</u>!

It is at this time that I heard of Stephen Hawking who was mentioned to be the next Albert Einstein. I can tell you now, as I look back at that period of the mid sixties and through the mid seventies, my faith in God was both challenged and very much strengthened. My faith was challenged because of the many areas of human reasoning that seemed to fit the rigorous discipline of logic and mathematics. On the other hand I was mesmerized by the overpowering evidence of the mysterious Hand of an <u>Omnipotent</u>, <u>Omniscient</u>, and <u>Omnipresent</u> Creator in the universe of nature!

I can tell you this; my many sleepless nights and reclusive days were rewarded by a closer glimpse at the masterpiece of God's Almighty Hand. I saw some of this mysterious cosmic picture in the language of Mathematics with its precision and elegance. I saw some of this through the meticulous details of Quantum Theory – a world where particles are so small but they contain and can release astounding levels of energy.

So back to Stephen Hawking. It was my admiration of his extraordinary intellect that made me perk up when I saw a piece in the New York Times back in June of 2006. The article caught my attention and I read it quickly and then read it again. Dr. Hawking was in Beijing, China presenting a paper, which the article briefly discussed. What caught my interest was the question that seems to keep "nagging" at my inquisitive mind. What is that question you ask?

Here was his "multiple" question:
- Why are we here?
- Where do we come from?
- Where are we headed?

I was baffled by his <u>multiple questions</u>! My baffle did not last for longer than it took for me to dictate to my secretary a respectful letter and send it registered mail to his Cambridge University address in London, England. What did you say to Dr. Hawking in your letter you are asking?

I clearly recalled stating my respect and admiration for his legendary intellect especially in areas of Theoretical Physics and Cosmology. I also said from reading his books and papers that he respected the thinking of others that may differ from his own views.

- To the question – "Where did we come from?" My answer: "We human species, are the progeny result of the creatural genius of the Creator God who the Bible describes in Genesis Chapter one and two."

- To the question – "Why are we here?" My answer: "We are here to propagate the species and progress toward a point in time when God will resume his intimate relationship with people in a global community. These are people who accept the Lord Jesus Christ as their personal Savior."

  To the question – "Where are we headed?" My answer: We are headed toward the fulfillment of the Biblical statement about of an unknown point in time when all of us on planet earth will head in two (2) directions. For specifics please refer to Matt. 7:13-14, *"Enter through the narrow gate. For wide is the gate and broad is the road that leads to destruction, and many enter through it. But small is the gate and narrow the road that leads to life, and only a few find it."*

This last question is the one that presents the greatest puzzle and challenge to Hawking's super intellect! Does it not surprise you that a person of Dr. Hawking's intelligence would not realize that questions that seem most difficult, or even unsolvable, have simple answers? Are you asking if the answer to the question where are we headed is in our handy reference Bible?

Yes my friend, I realize that although there are questions that will stubbornly refuse yielding to the most rigorous analysis of the brightest minds, The Bible never fails to present the final answer! The Bible passage in Matt. 7:13-14 echoes the words of Jesus who said: (paraphrase) there are two roads where we mortals travel, one wide and one narrow and they head toward two gates, one wide and one narrow. We have a choice on our journey. We may choose the broad road and the wide gate that head toward destruction. Jesus implored his listeners to head toward the narrow gate – the way to eternal life – the path of faith that leads to eternity. **Where we are headed depends on our choice**.

As I recap the gist of my letter to Dr. Hawking even now I pray sincerely that he would see the picture Jesus painted of eternity. My prayer also is that he would see these questions that baffle his brilliant mind are not subject to scientific analysis or the rigor of logic. My prayer again is that he would listen to Jesus who repeatedly offers eternal life to those who in simple faith call upon Him for mercy and grace.

Is that an answer to the question about the certainty of eternity? How about this verse in the words of our Lord Jesus: John 5:24

"Very truly I tell you, whoever hears my word and believes him who sent me has eternal life and will not be judged but has crossed over from death to life."

So, my friend about the certainty of eternity, we discussed earlier, what could be clearer and more certain than the words spoken by Jesus our Lord himself: (paraphrase) certainly, certainly, certainly, I say to you he that hears my words and believes on Him that sent Me has <u>eternal</u> life and will not be condemned but is passed from death to eternal life.

So there, plain, clear and simple is a declaration of the <u>certainty of eternity</u>, straight from the voice of Jesus our Lord. You say you need to gather your thoughts about the Stephen Hawking questions and the answers in my letter to him especially on the question about where are we headed? Ok! We are now heading toward the exit of Question Wonderland and we both show our surprise that time is passing so quickly. After this rest break, let's gather our thoughts to share some questions about ourselves.

CHAPTER 25

WHAT'S NEXT?

Ever been asked that question?

S ome questions that people ask you, and some questions that you ask people seem to come out of nowhere. They seem so strange because many times there are no expected answers. If you really think about it there are fewer times when you can or care to give an answer to those types of questions. One of these kinds of questions that come to mind is: What's Next? Is that a "trick" question or what?

I say trick because it gets you thinking that a few times you know the answer because you have planned to do something or say something in the next moments. How many times have we seen or heard of people who have had "next moments plans" that suddenly evaporate? That's the trick in the question – it's all about the future although the question

– "what's next?" seems to make room for events that could happen shortly because we seem to be in control of the near term events. What's next is really all about a future that is totally beyond the reach of our human senses. So what's next should really include the caveat "if God wills."

May I share with you a true story about a professor and a graduating student? The professor shall remain nameless and the graduating student we will call, Jim. This is commencement day on a university campus and student grads are brimming with nervous energy and various levels of mixed emotions. Professors, as usual, are scholarly in demeanor with a mix of calmness and thoughtfulness in their appearance. This graduation day is no different. The professor is sitting in his office awaiting signal to join the academic procession, when in walks Jim. He effusively greets his favorite professor and invites himself to a seat by the professor's desk.

As I recall the story, after the affectionate greeting by Jim, the professor fires this question at him! So Jim, its graduation day, and the day you have dreamed about and could hardly wait to see this big day arrive. So, what are you up to now? By the way, congratulations are in order! I was very pleased to grade your very impressive final paper in the honors program! Congrats again! So Jim, any job offers? Professor, I am glad you asked. I got my dream offer with a company that I am anxious to join and hopefully make a valuable contribution while I am there.

Then what's next? said the professor. Well, said Jim I'll work my way up as far as I can go and then, retire I guess! Then what's next? Said the professor. If I have a family, we will find a comfortable place to live out our lives, and then Jim paused to ponder his reply: "live out – the end of our days."

The professor then kindly asked, what about you Jim – this is personal about you – what's next? Professor, I never thought that far! What is next? I guess, like all other human beings – I'll pass on! That's what's next? The professor slowly asked. Again the professor said to Jim, so you really never thought that far out?

Jim said to the professor we don't have a lot of time and I certainly don't want you to miss your place in the commencement procession with your class. I am now going to ask you to not think of me as your professor for a moment and allow me to ask you a very personal question. Do you own a Bible? Yes sir, I do! Do you believe that the Bible gives us all the information and instruction we need to find a path from this life to the next? Yes sir, I do! Jim, if I showed you a passage or two from Scripture would you read it for information and instruction regarding what's next? You maybe surprised that I keep a Bible in my desk drawer said the professor.

So here Jim, is a verse in the New Testament – Gospel of John chapter 5 and verse 24: "Truly, truly, I tell you whoever hears my word and believes Him who sent me has everlasting life and will not be judged or condemned, but has crossed over from death to eternal life." So Jim, said the professor, here you have clear and simple information about hearing the Word of God, and also clear and simple information about what to do in order to be sure about what's next after your inevitable departure. There is the Certainty of a glorious eternity. This of course as the verse says, requires your choice and your faith – you are invited to believe the words of the Savior. Jim do you believe this declaration of Scripture? Yes sir, said Jim I do. I never thought of this very important matter with this kind of perspective. May I ask you a question professor said Jim in subdued tone? For me, right now in this office, what's next? So what is really your question – Jim? My question, professor is: what should I do next, right now? Well, if you will, we could pray together and you could simply express your faith as the verse says and be saved – God who remains eternally faithful – will keep His word. Would you like to join me in prayer? Let's pray! The professor prays this prayer with his student just before he makes his way to commencement.

> *"Lord, we come before you not as professor and student but as two sinners, one saved by your grace by accepting the Lord Jesus as Savior and the other who has just been awakened to the inevitable fact that faces all of us human mortals. I thank you for Jim's awareness that, no matter what we aspire in life, there comes a time that no mater who we are, where we are, what we have accomplished – we sometimes*

without any warning, must leave this life bounded by time and, cross the border into eternity."

As Jim submits his prayer of faith and his call upon the Lord Jesus for His grace and mercy in offering eternal salvation, he will start at this moment taking his first step into the new life – eternal life that Jesus clearly stated in the Bible verse we read together that said:

"Very truly I tell you, whoever hears my word and believes him who sent me has eternal life and will not be judged but has crossed over from death to life."
(John 5:24)

Jim, when I prayed a similar prayer many years ago, I did not understand much about the Bible, but I believed the Word of God and by God's matchless grace and my feeble faith – my life was dramatically changed. As the story ends, the professor and student hurried off to commencement exercises and agreed to keep in touch. For many, many reasons I resonate with this true story. I was particularly impressed that the student had the last question – **what should I do next**? A question that all of us without exception should ask with the sincerity that Jim did. Interesting isn't it that the answer he found that changed his life was exactly where we said that the answer to all QUESTIONS CAN BE FOUND! Remember? Well the moment we wish would never arrive is just a few minutes away. From here, I can see the exit from the **QUESTION WONDERLAND**. So just let's sit on this bench for a moment before we say farewell.

CHAPTER 26

SO LONG MY FRIEND!

Did you enjoy the question wonderland?

May I share a personal habit with you before we embrace with a farewell hug or high five if you prefer. It's my habit at the start or end of any trip I take, to say a brief prayer. Do you mind sharing this moment with me before we say goodbye? Ok?

Let's pray together. Lord I thank you for my partner and the opportunity to share some thoughts on a wide variety of questions. Most of all we are thankful for the acceptance of the Holy Scriptures as our answer resource for any questions we can ask or imagine. Finally, we thank you for reminding us, by reference to the Scriptures, that all of us, without exception, have limited time on this earth. Also, that all of us will enter eternity through one gate or the other. Also, that all of us have a choice regarding where we spend this existence

– called eternity. All of us can by faith respond to the entreaty of our Lord Jesus who implores us to enter into the "narrow" gate that leads to eternal life.

Lord, if my travel partner has not yet made the choice, I ask that as we part, something life-changing may happen as my partner reflects upon our conversation especially where and when it was simple and clear <u>what to do</u> and who to petition! As one who has made this petition i.e. calling on the name of the Savior and believing by faith the Gospel message and experiencing the New Birth and New Life, I leave the outcome of the opportunity in your hands. In the Name of our Lord Jesus I pray!

You say you want to pause for a few moments of silent prayer of your own. I respect that. I'll wait as long as it takes and then we will say a reluctant farewell.

If my travel partner is a fellow-believer may we share the joy that flavored this opportunity discussion while strolling through this Imaginary Question Wonderland? To God be the Glory! – **So long; farewell; adios; au revoir; das vidaniya; sayonara; andio; shalom; ajo; arrivederci; auf wiedersehen.**

EPILOGUE

I f you have been in the Question Wonderland with me by reading this book, I can't thank you enough for the pleasure of your company. The conversations about Questions were mentally insightful and stimulating.

If you have read my book titled "What are you Thinking" you may notice that I have an affinity for questions. Even as I am writing these closing comments, I am asking a few questions. I am wondering which comes first, the thoughts we think, or the questions we ask? Perhaps these two timeless questions go hand in hand and walk side by side. I'll leave that with you for your mental amusement.

Now that we have made our exit from the imaginary Wonderland, would you like to ask me: What is my question? My question is not simple but I assure you it is sincere. My question is not about probability or uncertainty but about **possibility!** Here is my question. How is it possible that the God who the Bible describes as the sole Creator and sustainer of this marvelous universe considers blessing a soul so unworthy as I? How is it possible that God, who although invisible, immortal, and dwells in unapproachable light and glorious majesty considers us? Why would He choose to bless us, why would He provide and make available such an all-inclusive salvation plan of blessings for us?

At the core of my repeated question is this: Why this blessing for me, a soul so unworthy of the least of His blessings? That's my question!

Until I find a better answer, I am going to say from the deepest reaches of my heart: it must be because of **His glorious grace, His incredible mercy, and His everlasting kindness.** Did that answer your question about what is my question?

Wherever you are in your life, whatever your experience, I hope you will take some quiet time with the Good Book, the Holy Bible in hand and ask some truly important questions – among them – Does God love and care for me? Do I really matter to God? Does He want me to have a personal relationship with Him? Why me? Why not me? The answers, my friend and travel partner, await you in the sacred pages of that ever-ready, all inclusive reference we shared during this unforgettable trip in the QUESTION WONDERLAND!

Sincerely, thanks again for the pleasure of your company.

POST SCRIPT
Last and First

I n the dedication statement of this book, I thought it was necessary but not sufficient to recognize George Verwer and Dale Rhoton co-founders of Operation Mobilization and their international team of missionaries.

On second thought, the dedication statement was not sufficient. In this Post Script, I repeat my thanks to George and Dale for their invaluable initiatives in facilitating the world-wide distribution of my book – "What are you Thinking!" Especially amazing is the roll-out that George triggered in India. Closer to home, George also arranged for thousands of books to be printed and distributed in Caribbean areas including radio promotions in Jamaica, West Indies. This was coordinated through the efforts of Harley Rollins and Pilot Press.

I mention this because the evidence of the Holy Spirit's movement among God's "SPECIAL FORCES" has been a spiritually enlightening and inspiring experience for me.

It has flavored and further inspired my writing this book – WHAT IS YOUR QUESTION. I am so thankful to God for bringing people like George and Dale in my path. They have become my dear friends, sharing a common passion for the worldwide spread of the Gospel.

So to George and Drena, Dale and Elaine, thanks beyond expression for your fellowship, help and encouragement. You were cited first in the Dedication, and last in the Postscript. Now I understand the meaning of the principle of LAST and FIRST stated by our Lord Jesus in Mark 10:31: "But many that are first shall be last and the last shall be first." You cover both extremities! For all the OMERS (operation mobilization team and supporters) I'll always remember my message aboard the Logos Hope, **a ship with a mission.** The message title still rings a daily reminder to me and I hope to you! By the way, the message title was: "**Remember to keep the Main Thing the Main Thing.**" I have not forgotten that and I hope no one does! God Bless!

CONVERSATION NOTES

Curiosity

CONVERSATION NOTES
Challenge

CONVERSATION NOTES

Creativity

Contact the Author

Nothing would be more pleasing than to hear from my "virtual" travelling companions who spent time with me in **Question Wonderland**.

I am honored to be currently serving in a pastoring ministry at Bible-centered Galilee Gospel Chapel in Queens, New York. I am also honored to serve as visiting professor at my alma mater at the City College of New York School of Engineering. So I am not really completely retired. Seems I am as busy as ever. Despite my activities you can be sure I'll be delighted to hear from you. Why? Just to hear what you are thinking about the questions we discussed!

Reach me at:

Phone (908) 464-1072

E-mail BGPCCNY@GMAIL.COM

APPENDIX 1

**Excerpts from our Conversation In
Question Wonderland**

From Curiosity:

- We are born with instincts that push our minds in directions of why, how, where, and what.
- There are no limits to our curiosity impulses – we just keep asking all kinds of questions.
- We are unique with this stubborn attribute of curiosity.
- Our civilization has progressed by climbing the ladders of endless curiosity questions and finding answers to most of them.

APPENDIX 2

Excerpts from Conversation In
Question Wonderland

From Challenge:

- There is an indomitable spirit in the core of man's being that pushes him to overcome challenges and not be overcome by them.
- There are no boundaries on land, sea or air that our generation of challenge questioners will not invade.
- The questions we face within ourselves are far more challenging than climbing Mount Everest. For example – the challenge of getting along – the very big question is "can we all get along?"
- Take the huge question of respectful tolerance, there are some nations, like our own in the USA, that provide for the practice of this social virtue. There are millions who have no tolerance for those who do

not believe or worship as they do. Why is this? This is an ancient question. We discussed the answer in Chapters 8 and 9.

- There were challenge questions that people like David Livingstone faced knowing that the odds of his survival were almost zero; yet he never backed down. He had a spiritual obsession about being his brother's keeper although his beneficiaries were complete strangers and continents apart from his native Scotland. Why not me, was his question.

- There were challenge questions that people like Winston Churchill was asked during World War II when the once mighty Britannia seemed to be at the mercy of Hitler's killing machines. Britain needed a leader who was never afraid of a challenge. The fact is – Churchill felt that when he appeared – challenge disappeared! When the urgent call came to Britain for a person to rise to the challenge of a somber moment in history – Churchill's legendary response – **NEVER! NEVER! NEVER!** – will not be erased from the pages of history.

APPENDIX 3

Excerpts from our Conversation In
Question Wonderland

From Creativity:

- In addition for man's insatiable quest into things and places unknown, he also does not shy away from questions about himself and about the seeming abstraction of God.

- In his creative inquisition, he asks who am I? Where did I come from? Where am I going? Our conversations skimmed the surfaces of these questions, but found the Bible always ready with answers.

- After the world famous cosmologist and theoretical physicist Steven Hawking's question on – where are we headed? We saw that in my letter to him on the subject of his question – the answer was clearly stated by our Lord Jesus Christ (Chapter 22).

- The question on "what's next" (Chapter 23) deserves a second read and perhaps more than a second thought, because it's real and personal. It's also surprising that many of us have not been "creative" enough to ask that question, but we should. Don't you think?

CPSIA information can be obtained at www.ICGtesting.com
Printed in the USA
BVOW11s1432200915

418728BV00001B/5/P